South Devon Walks with Children

Su Stewart

Published by Sigma Leisure – an imprint of
Sigma Press, 1 South Oak Lane, Wilmslow, Cheshire SK9 6AR, England.

British Library Cataloguing in Publication Data
A CIP record for this book is available from the British Library.

ISBN: 1-85058-590-3

Typesetting and Design by: Sigma Press, Wilmslow, Cheshire.

Cover photograph: Powderham Belvedere *(Su Stewart)*

Photographs: the author, except where indicated

Maps: Jeremy Semmens

Printed by: MFP Design & Print

Disclaimer: the information in this book is given in good faith and is believed to be correct at the time of publication. No responsibility is accepted by either the author or publisher for errors or omissions, or for any loss or injury howsoever caused. Only you can judge your own fitness, competence and experience.

Preface

This illustrated guidebook is primarily aimed at families with young children. A variety of twenty-five easy yet stimulating and enjoyable walks have been described, covering an area between Exeter in the East and Mount Edgecumbe (just over the Cornish border) in the West. The walks explore town and country, moorland, woodland and coast.

The format is such that this is an easy book to use. The routes are easy to follow and each walk has a concise introduction so that the reader can see at a glance whether the walk is suitable and will appeal to all members of the family.

The walks described are just a few of my favourite walks, and are by no means a comprehensive list of walks possible in this region (I think that would be a mind-boggling affair!). Trying to keep all members of a family entertained can be quite a task so I have included the odd story or legend and points of interest, such as local history or natural history. In addition, where appropriate I have included useful telephone numbers of local attractions which could combine well with the walk.

On a more practical note, you will find the location of the nearest toilets, refreshments and shops where available. Feasible pushchair routes are included where possible because, after all, if there is one, the baby must come too, and anyway, pushchairs are very handy for carrying picnic gear and coats, etc. This may prove useful for any members of the family in wheelchairs, although the book has not been written particularly with this in mind.

I have, apart from this introduction, tried to keep the text as brief as possible as when juggling with youngsters who want to be on the move, the last thing that is needed is to be forever stopping to read interminable lists of instructions.

No great walking experience is necessary, but by walking your way through this book you should gain both experience and a lot of fun, even for the most reluctant of children, or adults!

Su Stewart

Acknowledgements

Firstly, I would like to express my appreciation to Jamie for his limitless help and encouragement, not to mention his patience at being dragged out in all weathers on yet another walk. I want to thank Paul and Eileen Oakley and their sons, Peter and Russell, for being enthusiastic guinea pigs on several routes and returning with useful comments.

My thanks also to my friends and family who have accompanied me on exploratory walks and made helpful suggestions. We have had a few adventures in the process of researching this book. When Angie Abbott and her son, Joseph, came for "a nice little stroll", we got bogged down in mud and found level crossing gates locked, which provided good exercise trying to get pushchairs over. I decided not to include that route! Angie was not totally put off and came along on the Fingle Bridge walk with her husband Jeremy, Matthew aged seven, Kim aged five and two-year-old Joseph, all of whom managed the whole walk very well - which reassured me that my routes were not too ambitious for children. When poor Christine Connell came with us she slipped on ice and broke her arm! Yet she still persuaded me to have this book published. Nina Neal and her son, William, joined me in Dartmouth, Cockington and Widecombe with no traumas, so these routes have been duly included. Joy Retter and her children, Jason and Emma, introduced me to the excellent walk in Haldon. John and Sue Lyne and their sons, Henry and Joseph, showed me the Broadsands walk. Even my parents, mother-in-law, neighbour Sue and her baby, Ellie, have willingly come along to test out a number of walks.

I am grateful to Fiona Wells, Angie Abbott and Jamie Stewart for the photographs they took for me. Special thanks to both my parents for their help in research, local knowledge and grammar! Thanks also to Patrick Bell who sorted my word processor out and saved me from a crisis.

And last, but not least, a special mention for my son, Joel, for providing the inspiration for the book and, of course, accompanying me on every single walk.

Contents

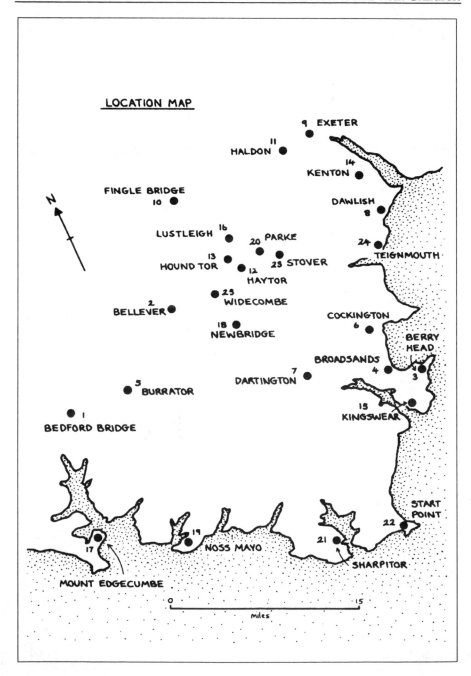

Before you begin...

Introductory notes on the text

This is a very unusual book, intended to be read by both parents and children. The following conventions have been used to make the book as useful as possible to both categories:

1. **Directions are numbered and appear in bold text so that they can be seen at a glance.**

☺ Information for the children is set in a contrasting typestyle. This is to be read aloud, or for them to read themselves. **OTHER INFORMATION FOR PARENTS APPEARS IN BOLD CAPITALS.**

In between the instructions you will often see text that looks like this. We have used this for all sorts of extra information, ranging from background material to escape routes – generally, the sort of thing you can skate over if you are in a rush to complete the main walk.

Checklists appear at the end of each walk, for the children to tick off things as they see them. If you do not want to write in the book, copy the checklist onto a piece of paper, and give one to each child, so that they can compete to see who spots the most.

Sketch maps

The maps are intended only as a rough guide to the route and are not drawn to scale. Unless otherwise stated north is upwards. Only buildings important to the route are shown. Numbers refer to the directions given in the text.

Roads = a continuous line
Footpaths = a dotted line
Trackways/forest roads/driveways = a line of dashes
Parking = P
Public house = PH

Quick reference chart

This chart allows you to plan your day at a glance, to check each route has the features or facilities you require. For more information on these see the individual route.

Notes

Public transport: Routes that are within a short walk from a bus stop.

Pushchairs: Walks with at least a small route suitable for pushchairs, though it may involve some effort.

Refreshments: café, tearoom or pub suitable for families along the route or within easy walking distance.

Terrain: what to expect in terms of ups and downs, type of path or track, and whether it turns muddy in poor weather.

Features: Places of specific interest to children along the route or close by.

Walk	Public Transport	Toilets	Push-chairs	Refresh-ments	Terrain	Total Distance	Features
1. Bedford Bridge	Bus	Yes	No	Ice cream van	Mostly flat tracks with one hill. Mud possible.	5 miles	River, woodland and mine workings
2. Bellever	Bus	Yes	With some difficulty	No	Rough tracks. Some hills. Mud possible.	3 miles	Dartmoor, woodland and river.
3. Berry Head	No	Yes	Yes	Café	Tracks and short stretch on road. Some hills. Mud possible.	2½ miles	Cliffs, sea birds, lighthouse, fortress remains with cannons.
4. Broadsands	Bus	Yes	Yes	Snacks	Paths and lane of gentle gradients. Mud possible.	1½ miles	Beaches, coastal and rural scenery.
5. Burrator	Bus nearby	Nearby with car	No. (Alternative supplied.)	Ice cream vans nearby with car.	Mostly tracks of gentle gradients. Mud possible.	3 miles	Dartmoor, woodland, leat, views of the reservoir.
6. Cockington	Bus	Yes	Yes	Cafés and pub	Easy paths and lanes of gentle gradients. All weather.	1½ miles	Picturesque village and parkland, lakes with fish and ducks, horses and carts.

Walk	Public Transport	Toilets	Push-chairs	Refresh-ments	Terrain	Total Distance	Features
7. Dartington	Bus	Yes	Yes	Cafes and snacks	Tracks or pavements of gentle gradients. Mud possible.	3 miles	Rural countryside, unusual shops, possible entertainment, beautiful garden.
8. Dawlish	Bus and train	Yes	Yes	Whole range	Paths and tracks flat except one steep short hill. Caution in rough weather.	4 miles	Beaches, trains, ducks, swans and shops.
9. Exeter	Bus	Yes	Yes	Whole range	All weather level paths and pavements. Mud possible	4 miles	Canal, river, boats, ducks, play areas and shops.
10. Fingle Bridge	Bus nearby	Yes	No	Pub and ice creams	Tracks. Some steep hills. Mud possible.	4 miles	Castle, ant hills woodland and river.
11. Haldon	No	No	No. (Alternative supplied.)	No	Paths and stepping stones. Some hills. Mud possible.	1½ miles	Woodland, stepping stones and tunnel. Birds of Prey view point.
12. Haytor	Bus	Nearby with car	With some difficulty.	Ice creams	Rough tracks and open moors with route finding easy except in fog. Some hills. Mud possible.	1¼ miles	Dartmoor. Tor and quarry lake. Extensive views as far as the sea.
13. Hound Tor	No	No	No	Some-times ice creams	Tracks. Some hills. Mud possible.	3½ miles	Dartmoor. Tors, river, woods, quarry, extensive views, ancient settlements.
14. Kenton	Bus	No	With some difficulty.	Pubs and shops	Paths and lanes, mostly level. Mud possible.	5 miles	Boats, trains. Deer, castle, estuary and birds.
15. Kingswear	Bus, train and ferries	Yes	Yes	Whole range	All weather paths and pavements, some hills.	3½ miles	Estuary, trains, boats, park, castle and shops.

Walk	Public Transport	Toilets	Push-chairs	Refresh-ments	Terrain	Total Distance	Features
16. Lustleigh	Bus	Yes	No	Cafes, pubs and grocery shops	Lanes and tracks. Some hills. Mud possible.	2½ miles	Pretty village, edge of Dartmoor, stream, woods, dramatic views.
17. Mount Edgecumbe	Bus and ferry	Yes	Yes	Café, pub and snacks	All weather paths. Some hills. Mud possible.	2½ miles	Beaches, gardens, ferry crossing, ducks, geyser and camellias.
18. Newbridge	No	Yes	Part of route.	Ice creams	Rough tracks, some hills. Mud possible.	3 miles or 4 miles.	River, woods, canoes in winter, ponies.
19. Noss Mayo	Bus	Yes	With some difficulty.	Pubs and small shops	Country lanes and footpaths. Some hills. Mud possible.	4 miles	Pretty fishing village, boats, fine coastal views.
20. Parke	Bus	No	Yes	No	Tracks, mostly level. Mud possible.	2 miles	River, old railway, woods, maze, cycling possible for part of this route.
21. Sharpitor	Bus nearby	No	No	No	Rough tracks, some hills. Mud possible.	2 miles	Dramatic coastal scenery, beach, optional trip to National Trust museum.
22. Start Point	No	No	Short part of route.	No	Coastal footpath, some hills. Mud possible.	2½ miles	Lighthouse, dramatic coastal scenery, beach, optional scramble.
23. Stover	Bus	Yes	Yes	Ice creams	Paths and tracks, level. Mud possible.	4 miles	Woods, lakes, waterways, ducks and other wildlife.
24. Teignmouth	Bus and train	Yes	Yes	Snacks and ice creams	Flat path with an exposed drop in parts. Caution in rough weather.	2½ miles	Beach, coastal views, trains, red cliffs, sea side attractions.
25. Widecombe	Bus	Yes	No. (Alternative supplied.)	Tea rooms, pubs and shops in Wide-combe	Rough tracks, mostly clearly defined. Hills. Mud possible.	2½ miles	Dartmoor with dramatic views and Tors.

The Country Code – and other commonsense advice

Here are a few words of advice, partly based on the Country Code, to help you and others.

☆ Guard against fire. If the countryside is dry just one spark can cause a serious fire. Even a piece of glass could start a fire if the sun shines through it onto dry vegetation.

☆ Fasten all gates. It is important to leave gates as you find them so that animals do not stray.

☆ Keep dogs under proper control. If there are any farm animals around, particularly sheep, dogs should be on a lead. It is also advisable to keep dogs on leads on roads to protect them and others.

☆ Keep to paths across farm land. By walking across fields you could damage the crops and anger the farmer.

☆ Avoid damaging fences, hedges and walls. Remember that they are someone else's property and that they are there for a reason, for example, to keep animals in or out.

☆ Leave no litter – take it home unless there is a bin provided. Litter can spoil a beautiful area for others and can also be very dangerous to wildlife. Perhaps you could do the countryside a good turn and pick up litter, but children would need supervising in this.

☆ Safeguard water supplies. Do not pollute any waterway.

☆ Protect wildlife, plants and trees. It is illegal to dig up any wild flowers – if everyone were to do this, there would eventually be none. It is forbidden to feed the Dartmoor ponies, partly because it does them no good, and even more because it attracts them to roads where they are at risk of being knocked down by cars. They can also become a nuisance, terrorising unsuspecting picnickers.

☆ Take care on country roads. Walk on the right-hand side so that you are facing oncoming traffic. Walk in single file and keep to the side on narrow lanes, holding on to young children.

☆ Respect the life of the countryside. Do not disturb others by making too much noise. Leave the countryside as you found it.

☆ Be aware that wild animals and farm animals, however cute, can bite or trample.

☆ Beware of electric fences. These could give a nasty shock. If in any doubt whether it is an electric fence, don't touch it. They are usually single wires held up by occasional plastic supports. They are used to keep farm animals in a particular area.

☆ Exercise caution near water, cliffs, roads and railways.

☆ Never eat wild berries or fungi. Most adults will be able to identify blackberries and wild strawberries, but if in doubt, do not touch. There are some very good pocket guides for sale which will help you identify plants and animals and increase the interest and enjoyment of the walk.

☆ Go properly prepared for the weather, the terrain and unexpected eventualities. The correct clothing and footwear will ensure that you will enjoy the walk all the more, and will not suffer later. Take sun hats in summer and woolly hats in winter. Light layers are best as they are easily carried.

☆ If any sore patches develop on the feet, put a plaster on as soon as possible to prevent a blister forming.

☆ It is most important to protect against the sun, as well as against the cold and the rain.

☆ Go prepared with snacks or treats in case you are out for longer than anticipated, they can also be a useful incentive!

☆ If possible, take an Ordnance Survey map with you.

☆ Keep a first aid kit in your car.

☆ If you are walking in a remote area, it is wise to tell someone where you are going and how long you will be, remembering to tell them when you are back.

☆ Do not leave valuables in your car, particularly in remote spots.

☆ When walking through bracken or long grass it is wise to wear long trousers tucked into socks as protection against ticks as the bites can sometimes cause illness.

☆ If you do find yourself confronted with mud or sand when with a pushchair, pulling it backwards is much easier.

☆ Encourage the children to spot things or find the route to keep them interested.

☆ Carry a light rucksack, or plastic bag in a pocket, for collecting things such as blackberries, pine cones, shells, etc.

1. Bedford Bridge to Double Waters

This walk takes you along the picturesque Walkham valley as far as Double Waters, the meeting place between the River Walkham and the River Tavy. There are many beautiful picnic spots and ideal places for paddling. This part of the valley was an important mining area in the 1800s so you will see the entrances to mines with their spoil heaps and derelict buildings.

Starting point:	Bedford Bridge. The car park is free. Bedford Bridge is on the A386 between Yelverton and Tavistock, about 1 mile from Horrabridge.
Car park map reference:	504703
Distance:	About 5 miles
Terrain:	Well defined tracks, some liable to be muddy. Mostly flat, with one hill.
Maps:	OS Landranger 201, Plymouth and Launceston
By bus:	For further details phone 01752 222666.
Public Toilets:	Open in the summer at Bedford Bridge.
Refreshments:	In the summer there may be ice cream vans at Bedford Bridge.
Telephone Box:	At the entrance to the car park
Pushchairs:	Not possible

1. **Join the path at the end of the car park. The path goes through woodland adjacent to the river and then drops down to the river.**

☺ You will pass a number of derelict buildings connected with the mining activities of Wheal Franco. Wheal Franco was worked between 1823 and 1870. In 1857 this was one of Devon's most productive mines, producing substantial amounts of copper ore. The old engine shaft went down 160 fathoms (almost 300 metres).

Look out for wildlife such as wagtails, wrens and squirrels. In the damp ground near the river, in the summer, you may find the

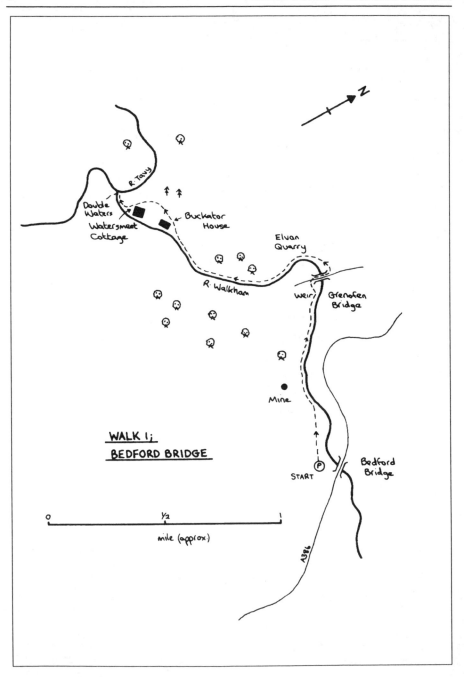

Z

R. Tawy

Double
Waters

Watersmeet
Cottage

Buckator
House

Elvan
Quarry

R. Walkham

Weir

Grenofen
Bridge

Mine

WALK 1;
BEDFORD BRIDGE

START

P

Bedford
Bridge

A386

0   ½   1

mile (approx.)

pretty yellow monkey flower, so named because it looks like a grinning face. This plant originated in Alaska, but thrives in wet conditions.

There is a mine shaft or 'adit' to your left, which is fenced off for safety.

☺ Further on there is a broken weir with a dry leat and other features next to it. These are the remains of Poldice Mine, worked in the 1880s for small yields of copper, lead and tin. There was once a water wheel here. Up to your left is Sticklepath Wood. "Stickle" means steep so this is an aptly named wood.

2. **The path by the river will take you to a car park beside Grenofen Bridge. To reach this car park when travelling along the A386 towards Tavistock, turn left at the Half Way Inn.**

☺ Grenofen Bridge was once important as it carried the main route from Tavistock to Buckland Monachorum.

3. **Cross the bridge. Turn left just after the bridge through a gate onto a public bridleway.**

☺ On the downstream side of the bridge is a deep pool where you might be able to see some fish.

You will come to a wall of rocks to your right which hides a 19th-century elvan quarry. Elvan is a local rock which was once used for building. It has the useful characteristic of being soft to cut out from underground and to work, and then hardening as it dries. It was, therefore, used for carvings on buildings. The Romans made pots out of elvan.

This is a very pretty stretch of river with rapids and is a great area for exploring. Look for a miniature gorge with its little waterfalls, and formations caused by rocks swirling around creating holes in the river bed.

The woods are mixed deciduous, with lichen thriving on some of the trees and with bracken, gorse and foxgloves on the ground. Ponies and sheep graze in the shelter of the woodland.

There is a well-preserved mine chimney on your right. There are lots of mine buildings and several adits leading into the hillside. This was West Down Mine, a copper mine. The copper ore would have been shipped from Morwellham Quay to South Wales to be crushed and smelted.

If you have an interest in the mining activities, then Morwellham Quay is an excellent place to visit with fun for all the family. For further details phone 01822 832766.

4. **The track comes up to a house called Buckator. Go around the back of the house to your left. The track climbs up at this point and goes away from the river.**

😊 Buckator was once the mine captain's house.

West Down Mine chimney

5. **Take the left fork off the main track, following the direction of the wall back down to the river and passing Watersmeet Cottage on your left. Rejoin the track by the river, heading downstream. When you see a small rocky hill ahead of you, take the track between the rocks at the top.**

😊 Here you are greeted by the River Tavy.

6. **Explore the Double Waters area at your leisure.**

😊 The house perched on a hill by the river is the mine captain's house of the Virtuous Lady Mine. Around here you will see the spoil heaps from this copper mine. It is said that the mine was named after the first Queen Elizabeth. This mine was particularly active in the mid-19th century, but was last worked in the 1870s when the price of copper dropped. At this time the mine was being worked to a depth of 20 fathoms (36 metres) and employing about 40 people. You may notice that there are not many plants growing on the spoil heaps. This is because of the arsenic in the soil. Arsenic is a substance which is a by-product of the copper and tin mining process. Arsenic is a poison which kills plants as well as animals. It was used in the manufacture of paint, dyes and glass, as well as insecticide and weed-killer and in medicine. At the end of the copper mining era, attention was paid to the arsenic which was readily available from these dumps.

7. **Return by the same route.**

If the route described is too long, it would be feasible to start the walk at Grenofen Bridge and to walk either the upper or lower sections of the walk. Grenofen Bridge map reference: 490709.

Checklist

☐ A sheep

☐ A squirrel

☐ A Dartmoor pony

☐ A fish

☐ Lichen

☐ A mine chimney

☐ A buzzard

☐ A wagtail

2. Bellever Forest

Bellever is just about in the centre of Dartmoor so you really get the feel of this immense, rugged and wild landscape. The walk takes you through the conifer plantations and then up to Bellever Tor with its superb views, before heading back to the beautiful river and clapper bridge.

Starting point:	Car park for Bellever Forest, which is south from Post-bridge.
Car park map reference:	656773
Distance:	About 3 miles
Terrain:	Wide forestry tracks, rough, stony tracks and short-cropped moorland. Various inclines but nothing too demanding. Some parts could be muddy in wet weather.
Maps:	OS Outdoor Leisure 28, Dartmoor
By bus:	For details phone 01752 222666.
Public Toilets:	At the car park, including a toilet for the disabled and baby changing facilities.
Refreshments:	None. This is a very good place to bring a picnic!
Pushchairs:	Not possible for the route described. There are other tracks in the forest where pushchairs could go quite a distance.

1. **Start from the far end of the car park. Go off towards the right, through a gate and up the slope, following the red route.**

☺ This is a working forest, so you may see or hear the forestry workers at work, or at least evidence of this with the neatly stacked piles of logs and recently felled trees. The original planting was done in 1921, and as trees are felled so new ones are planted in their place. The Forestry Commission bought the forest from the Duchy of Cornwall in 1931. Bellever Forest covers about 565 hectares/1400 acres.

You will get views of Bellever Tor above, to your right.

2. **Following the red markers, you will turn right down a slope**

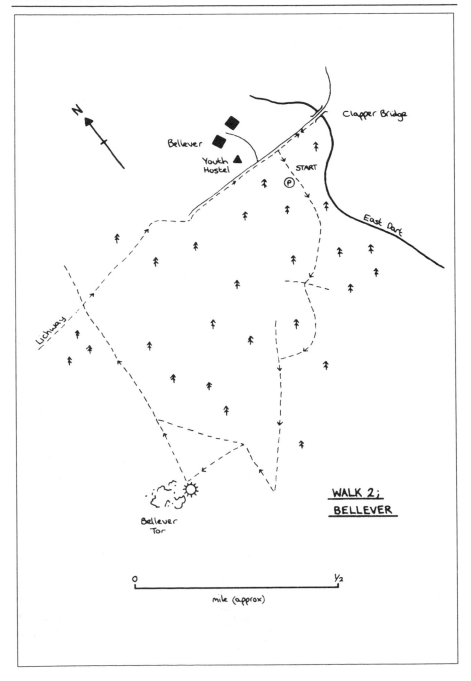

N

Clapper Bridge

Bellever

Youth
Hostel

START

P

East Dart

Lichway

WALK 2;
BELLEVER

Bellever
Tor

0   ½

mile (approx)

and across a stream, and then climb again to a T-junction with a bench for a welcome rest.

☺ Now to your right are views of the open moor, and you are walking amongst young trees, bracken and foxgloves. Foxgloves are named from the Anglo-Saxon words for little people's bells. They are important plants as they have been used through the ages for the drug digitalin which is used for heart complaints. It is interesting watching the bees as they visit each flower in turn, from the bottom to the top.

3.   **At this T-junction you will lose the yellow markers which are for the shorter route back to the car park to your right. For our route, follow the red markers to your left. The track will change direction to your right, and the views will get increasingly good as you climb.**

4.   **At the next junction, turn left up a rough track and continue straight ahead and up for Bellever Tor.**

It is possible to miss out the Tor by following the red markers, but this would be a great shame.

Bellever Tor

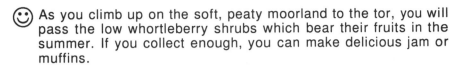 As you climb up on the soft, peaty moorland to the tor, you will pass the low whortleberry shrubs which bear their fruits in the summer. If you collect enough, you can make delicious jam or muffins.

The views from the tor, with its trig point, are terrific. Starting from the north and going clockwise you can see the following tors: Hartland, Birch, Honeybag, Hay, Rippon, Yar, Laughter in the foreground and Sharp behind, North Hessary, Great Mis, Beardown, Longaford, Crow, Higher White, Lower White and Sittaford. Dartmoor covers 365 square miles.

Below, in the direction of Longaford Tor, you can see the Powder Mills, where gunpowder was manufactured in the 19th century. It did well until its closure in the 1890s, when the use of gunpowder for mine and quarry blasting was overtaken by dynamite.

Laughter Tor may take its name from the pixies who are said to make merry there. If you should see them, keep quiet in case they make you join in until you are utterly exhausted, as they once did to a farmer called Tom White from the Postbridge area. He never went out on the moors at night again!

Bellever is a beautiful tor, with its jointed granite formations. At the top you are at a height of 1,456 feet/475 metres above sea level.

Up until the 1930s, there was a day in May known as Bellever Day which was a popular event marking the end of the hunting season. There were picnics, organised races and side stalls selling food and drinks. Hundreds of Dartmoor people gathered here.

5. **Descend from the tor on the wide, peaty track to the north-east until you reach the edge of the forest and pick up the red markers again.**

Enjoy the views as you go, but beware of the peaty dips in the path on the way. In areas of the moor with poor drainage, and, of course, relatively high rainfall, the ground can become waterlogged so that the plants do not decompose in the normal way but build up into peat instead. The depth of peat on the moor varies from a few inches to up to 4 metres. At one time peat was cut from the moors and used as a fuel, but this practice would be forbidden now. The peat was used in homes and also in the tin industry.

6. Enter the forest again, following the red markers.

☺ The fast growing Sitka Spruce is the most common species of the forest. It originated in north-west America and thrives in the wet and windy Dartmoor climate. You may also see the Japanese Larch which is a deciduous conifer so is most attractive in the Spring and Autumn. The Sitka Spruce can be identified by its sharp, pointed needles with a bluish colour on the underside, whereas the Japanese Larch has needles in clusters. Listen to the wind in the trees.

7. At the junction with the Lichway, follow the red markers to the right and walk downhill on the Lichway.

☺ The Lichway is a medieval track used by the people of this area to take their dead to burial, and to attend church services in Lydford. This was in force until 1260, when they were then to go to Widecombe instead. The Lichway was still used for many centuries as Lydford was an important centre with its market, prison, castle and law courts.

Particularly in the autumn, this is a good spot for fungi so bring along an identification book if possible so that you can identify **but not pick**. There is a variety of wildlife living in the forest: stoats, weasels and squirrels; roe or red deer; owls, buzzards and sparrow-hawks; blackbirds, jays and magpies and many others.

8. Go through the gate at the bottom of the track. Pass the farm and then the youth hostel and you should meet the road.

☺ Passing the farm, you may spot tractors and redundant tractor wheels.

9. Before returning to the car park, it is well worth walking down the road to see the river and clapper bridge. If you wish, you can walk back to the car from the river through the woods.

☺ The clapper bridge is medieval, and is not complete, but well worth a look, as is the larger clapper bridge at nearby Postbridge. Clapper bridges are made of huge pieces of unwrought granite and were used by packhorses.

The East Dart River at Bellever is idyllic for paddling, fishing for minnows and tadpoles, and for picnics, but you might find you are not the only one with this in mind at the height of the summer.

☺ There are usually groups of ponies grazing near the bridge.

Checklist

☐ Peat

☐ A pine cone

☐ A jay

☐ A water boatman

☐ A tadpole or frog

☐ A Dartmoor pony

☐ A cow

☐ A tractor

3. Berry Head

Berry Head Country Park is a conservation area of great note, with its
rare plant species associated with the limestone cliffs, and also the
large breeding colonies of sea birds. The cliffs of around 60
metres/200 feet high are as impressive as you could imagine, and on
clear days you will have views of Torbay, Lyme Bay and Dartmoor.
You will explore some Napoleonic forts and see a working lighthouse.

Starting point:	Pay and display car park in Berry Head Country Park. On reaching Brixham, follow the brown signs to Berry Head. There is a display centre at the car park.
Car park map reference:	941563
Distance:	About 2½ miles
Terrain:	Well-defined tracks, could be muddy in places in wet weather. Some hills.
Maps:	OS Landranger 202, Torbay and South Dartmoor
Public Toilets:	Next to the car park
Refreshments:	On sale during the season in the Old Guardhouse in the Northern Fort.
Pushchairs:	Possible for the whole route. A double pushchair would manage the area around the Northern Fort, but not the whole route as the tracks become too narrow in places.

1. **At the top of the car park, follow the signs to the lighthouse and
   Northern Fort.**

☺ Near the car park is a strange-looking structure with an even
stranger name – The Berry Head DVOR. This is an air traffic
navigation aid – Doppler VHF Omni-directional Range. How's
that for a mouthful!

The Napoleonic forts are interesting to explore, and to imagine
what it must have been like for the men living in them – pretty
grim I would think! The cannons are worth looking at. To find out
more, there are some information boards at the fort.

There was once a Saxon fortification on the same site but this

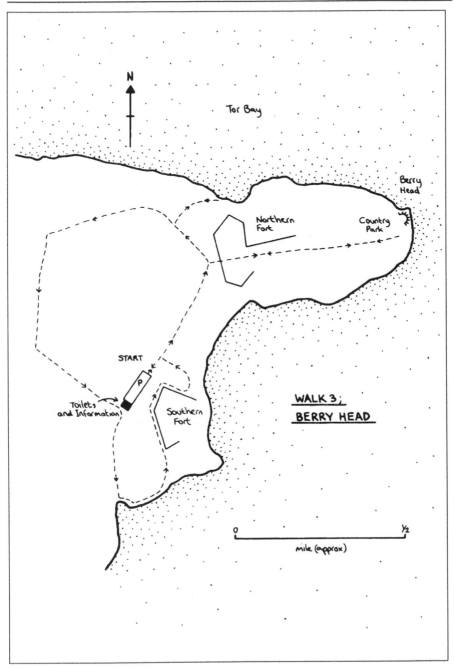

Tor Bay

N

Berry
Head

Northern
Fort

Country
Park

START

P

Toilets
and Information

Southern
Fort

WALK 3;
BERRY HEAD

0   ½
mile (approx)

has long since become obscured. The word "berry" is the Saxon word for "fortification".

You will walk through the Northern Fort and along a track with exposed limestone showing through, until you reach the lighthouse with its revolving light and reflective prisms. This lighthouse does not need to be tall as it is already 60 metres/200 feet above sea level.

Berry Head lighthouse was built in 1906. In 1921 it was converted to acetylene and then modernised and converted to mains electricity in 1994. It is the smallest and highest lighthouse in Britain.

The optic was originally turned by a weight falling down a 45m-deep shaft — but now a motor is used. The light flashes every 15 seconds and has the brightness of 9,000 candles. It's light can be seen 14 miles out to sea.

Just beyond the lighthouse is a rock with an orientation compass so that you can identify the local landmarks.

Berry Head lighthouse

2. **The cliffs are just beyond the lighthouse and are extremely impressive, but as they are unfenced, EXTREME CAUTION MUST BE EXERCISED.**

☺ You may see birds such as fulmars, razorbills, kittiwakes and gulls nesting in nooks and crannies in the cliff or soaring above and below. There could be some intrepid climbers scaling the cliffs, with a wet landing awaiting them if they fall off. One of these climbs has the evocative name of "Magical Mystery Tour". Rather them than me! Out to sea there are usually plenty of boats — yachts and kayaks, fishing boats from Brixham, or perhaps tankers using the bay for shelter. On a clear day it is possible to see as far as Portland Bill which is 45 miles away, and you can also look back towards Dartmoor.

3. **Return to the entrance of the Northern Fort and take the track on the right towards Brixham. Shortly, on your right, there is a gate. Go through the gate and follow the track to the bottom of the huge quarry which is below the Northern Fort.**

☺ The limestone has been extensively quarried for building purposes. At the bottom of the track, by the sea, is a popular spot for fishing.

This cliff would have been formed under the sea millions of years ago, before the sea level dropped. On top of the headland you may have noticed how flat it was. This is a very good example of a wave cut platform. Berry Head may look absolutely huge, but it is actually getting smaller each year with the action of the waves.

4. **Return to the main track and continue down in the direction of Brixham. The track will become a bit rough and possibly muddy as it goes through a little wood. Ignore the steps heading off to the right, but take the left fork until you reach a stile with the road on the other side. Go up the hill on your left and continue until you reach the car park.**

☺ Just below the entrance to the quarry you will pass a gun bed with some seats and superb views of Brixham Harbour and the bay.

5. **At the Berry Head Centre end of the car park, follow the road a short distance before joining the St. Mary's Bay footpath sign.**

This track is narrow, bumpy and liable to be muddy so is not suitable for double pushchairs.

6. **When you reach the sea, take the left footpath to the Southern Fort, following wooden stakes with acorn pictures on them. Follow the track around the edges and eventually into the fort, and then down the hill to the car park.**

☺ Before you reach the car park, you will pass a notice board identifying some of the sea birds you may see.

There are benches and picnic tables in various parts of the park, and plenty of room for running about, letting off steam. You may see model aeroplanes and kites flying.

As this is a conservation area, it is important to leave it as you found it.

Checklist

☐ A cannon

☐ A fulmer

☐ A tanker ship

☐ A sailing boat

☐ A model aeroplane

☐ A fisherman

☐ A weather vane

☐ A telescope

4. Broadsands

If you like beaches, sea views, steam trains and cows, then this short coastal and countryside walk is for you.

Starting point:	From the Paignton to Brixham Road, turn into Broadsands Road, going under the viaduct and parking in the Broadsands Beach pay and display car park.
Car park map reference:	896572
Distance:	About 1½ miles
Maps:	OS Landranger 202, Torbay and South Dartmoor area
By bus:	For details phone 01752 222666
Terrain:	Either flat or gentle slopes on paths or lanes. Could be muddy in places in wet weather.
Public Toilets:	At the car park
Refreshments:	Ice creams, along with beach paraphernalia, sold in a shop at the car park.
Telephones:	At the car park
Pushchairs:	Possible for the whole route except going down on to the beach at Elberry Cove.

1. **Walk to the promenade and turn right. Go through the kissing gate and follow the path signed to Elberry Cove. This path takes you across part of the Churston Golf Course. Go through the cycle prevention barrier and follow the coast around to Elberry Cove.**

☺ Near the car park is a small reed-bed which attracts birds such as reed and sedge warblers, black caps, willow warblers and chiffchaffs.

Broadsands beach is a popular beach with a large expanse of red sand, ideal for building sand castles and for paddling. Out to sea you can watch people enjoying various water sports. Surrounding the beach is a colourful array of beach huts. Behind the beach are two railway viaducts, Broadsands and Hookhills, along which, in the summer, you may see the steam trains as they puff along between Paignton and Kingswear.

Broadsands beach

On Wednesday, 10th January 1866, a hurricane struck, wrecking 41 boats in the bay, 7 at Broadsands and leaving 73 dead.

Once you have passed through the kissing gate, you will be walking along the lower edge of Churston Golf Course. You will now get superb views of Torbay, over to Torquay and towards Berry Head Breakwater ahead of you. As you round the headland you will see the beautiful blue-green waters of Elberry Cove. It is quite likely that you may see some water-skiing taking place.

2. **Go down to the beach at Elberry Cove by the steps, and then either back up the same steps or up a very steep dirt track. The beach is of steeply sloping, large pebbles. TAKE CARE NOT TO TWIST YOUR ANKLE ON THESE.**

☺ In the 19th century, Elberry Cove was the bathing beach of Lord Churston. You can still see the remains of his bath house, which is said to be an early form of sauna. There are remains of large coppers and several fireplaces.

In the woods at Elberry you may see the butcher's broom plant with its evergreen, spiky-tipped, oval "leaves". This is a strange plant with no true leaves, but flattened stems instead. It has

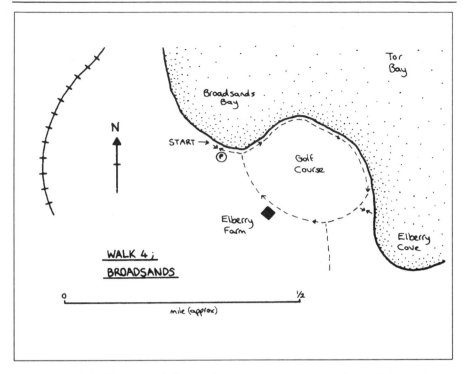

WALK 4;
BROADSANDS

greenish flowers followed by large red berries. It is named because it was traditionally used to sweep butchers' blocks. It was once also used as a medicine to help knit broken bones.

3.   Rejoin the path and head towards Broadsands, bearing around to the right and passing Elberry Farm on your left.

☺ You are now in pleasant countryside and it would be easy to forget how near you are to the sea, and taking a peek through the hedges on your left you will see that the path runs along the edge of a modern housing estate.

As you pass Elberry Farm look out for the assortment of tractors and farm equipment, not to mention an old ambulance and a boat. In a field behind these sheds there seems to be a sort of grave yard for pedaloes. The farm, which sells fresh eggs, honey and vegetables, looks quite old with narrow slits in the walls of red sandstone. Often you will get the chance to see the cows and calves in the farmyard or the fields.

4. The bottom of this lane takes you into the car park. You could
    extend the walk by going along the promenade in the direction
    of Saltern Cove, and then back to the car park along the beach
    for a paddle.

Checklist

☐ A cow

☐ A tractor

☐ A shell

☐ A steam train

☐ A water skier

☐ A sailing boat

☐ An old ambulance

☐ A golfer

5. Devonport Leat, Burrator

In my opinion the Burrator area is a good example of how man can actually enhance the natural beauty of the landscape. During this walk you will travel beside the Devonport Leat and the River Meavy through woods and open moorland. You will see ruined farmhouses and old tin workings, and even water flowing uphill!

Starting point:	Park at Cross Gate. You will find it on the map by looking between Burrator Reservoir and Leather Tor. From Yelverton, take the Princetown road B3212. Go through Dousland and take the right hand turning after about three quarters of a mile, just after a patch of woodland also on your right. Follow this road, turning left at the Y-junction, and continue to Cross Gate, distinctive for its superb views of the reservoir and its stone cross beside the leat that looks a bit like a T.
Car park map reference:	562695
Distance:	About 3 miles
Terrain:	Mostly well-defined tracks with one section over rough ground which could be boggy in places. Flat or gentle slopes.
Maps:	OS Outdoor Leisure 28, Dartmoor
By bus:	To Burrator Dam. For further details phone 01752 222666.
Public Toilets:	Nearest are at the Burrator Dam
Refreshments:	During popular times there are usually ice cream vans at the dam or at Norsworthy Bridge.
Pushchairs:	Not possible for this route. At the end of this description I shall outline a suggestion or two.

1. **From the car park, follow the leat upstream on its left. As you start to walk you get good views of Down Tor ahead and Leather Tor above you to the left.**

☺ There are wonderful views of Burrator Reservoir from Cross Gate. Burrator Reservoir was built between 1893 and 1898 to supply the Plymouth area with water. In May and June the edges

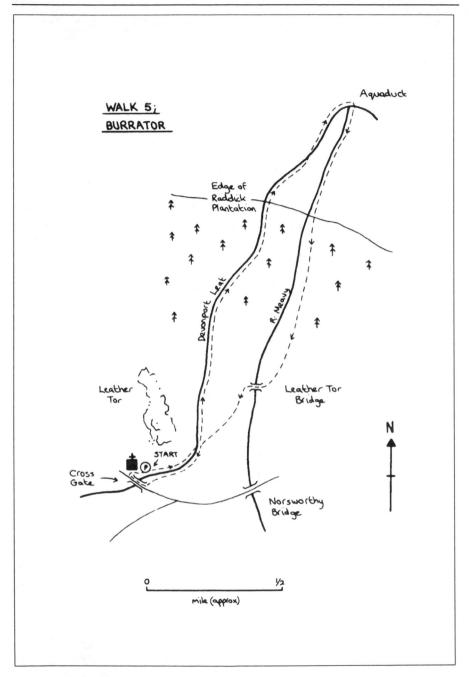

WALK 5;
BURRATOR

Aquaduct

Edge of
Raddick
Plantation

Devonport Leat

R. Meavy

Leather
Tor

Leather Tor
Bridge

START

Cross
Gate

Norsworthy
Bridge

N

0   ½
mile (approx)

of the reservoir are brightened up with the rhododendrons and azaleas.

You can't miss the distinctive headless granite cross. This is Lowery Cross and is one of the series of medieval crosses which marks the monastic route between Buckfast Abbey and Tavistock. Look for the cairn on your left.

2. Cross the leat and continue upstream on its right bank.

☺ The Devonport Leat was built in the 1700s to supply Devonport with water. Its water comes from the Cowsic, West Dart and Blackabrook rivers and starts near Wistmans Wood. It goes through one tunnel of 592.5 metres and travels over several aqueducts. In 1891, during a blizzard, Devonport had no water supply for several days. Problems such as this, as well as increased demand, precipitated the building of the reservoir. The leat is 15 miles long by the time it reaches the reservoir. It was built by French prisoners of war from Princetown and cost £23,400 to build.

Look for fish, damsel and dragon flies.

3. Cross the stile and continue beside the leat until you leave the forest.

☺ This is mainly a coniferous forest, but you can still find rowan, birch and sycamore. Look for flowers such as potentilla, knapweed, Himalayan balsam and heather. Every so often there are single granite clapper bridges crossing the leat.

4. As you leave the woods, walk through the ruins of Stanlake Farm and rejoin the leat. Walk along its left bank to the aqueduct. Ahead of you is the mast of North Hessary Tor.

☺ Explore the ruins of the farm then take a close look at the leat as you walk to the aqueduct. Look at the step weirs in the leat as it runs downhill, along the route you will also see various sluice gates used for regulating the flow. On the other bank you can see the spoil heaps of the old tin workings. The pipeline which enters the leat just downstream of the aqueduct is the point at which water flows uphill. It supplies about half a million gallons/2,273 litres of water per day from the River Meavy to supplement the leat.

☺ Above the aqueduct the water flows down a steep slope as a cascade. I have visited this place in freezing conditions and it was spectacular with vertical icicles looking like giant thermometers as the ice covered the grasses.

5. **From the aque-duct, follow the rough track on the left bank of the River Meavy as it flows down-stream, to the edge of the forest.**

☺ You will now be walking amongst the spoil heaps.

The aqueduct (Fiona Wells)

The ground is rough and liable to be boggy, with springs visible. If the ground is too wet at this point, it would be wise to return back by the outward route beside the leat.

☺ Here there are some miniature versions of feather-bed bogs, so named as they wobble as you walk across them.

6. **Cross the stile into the forest and follow the track to Leather Tor Bridge. Do not cross the river until you reach Leather Tor Bridge.**

☺ Leather Tor Bridge is a relatively modern clapper bridge, the last of its type built on Dartmoor, at the cost of £12.10s in 1833. Downstream from the bridge is a ford. This is where the path known as the Abbots Way crosses the River Meavy. The monks would have come this way between Tavistock and Buckland Abbeys and Buckfast Abbey. The bridge was destroyed in the 1950s by a flood, and then reassembled by the Plymouth Corporation.

7. **Cross Leather Tor Bridge and follow the track to Cross Gate which is signposted near the ruins of Leather Tor Farm.**

☺ On your right, as the track climbs away from the river, you will see a cave. This is known as a potato cave. These are found in various locations over Dartmoor and were dug out of the rotted soft granite known as growan. Growan is firm enough so that the roof will stay up, and has good drainage, ideal for the storage of vegetables. It is said to have been used by smugglers, too.

Just up from the potato cave you can see the ruined farm, which you can look at if you cross the stile, but take care because of possible loose stones. The farms of Stanlake and Leather Tor were evacuated before the heightening of the Burrator Dam in 1928.

8. **If you wish, instead of crossing the leat when you reach it, you can follow a narrow path on its left bank to return to Cross Gate. Keep on the track beside the leat, do not veer to the left. You will find yourself crossing an old-style stile, a rather rickety affair.**

Checklist

☐ A stone cross

☐ A television transmission ariel

☐ A clapper bridge

☐ A sluice gate

☐ A damsel or dragonfly

☐ A potato cave

☐ A clapper bridge

☐ A bog

Alternatives for pushchairs

From Sheepstor Dam

This is a flat walk away from the crowds. You may see the odd fishing boat and perhaps some Canadian geese. Look for squirrels, tadpoles, frogs, butterflies and birds such as woodpeckers.

Starting point:	Park the car in the small car park beside the reservoir, north of Sheepstor Dam.
Map reference:	557681
Distance:	About 1 mile
Terrain:	Flat tracks, possibly liable to be muddy but rarely prohibitive.

Cross the wooden stile (easy manoeuvre with two adults to lift a pushchair). Follow the path, with the lake on your right, across Sheepstor Dam and on towards Burrator Dam. The path ends on a small headland. Retrace your steps to the car.

☺ Ahead of you at the start of this walk you can hear a waterfall. This is actually the Devonport Leat as it cascades out of a metal pipe. This walk affords you superb views of the reservoir and surrounding moors. At the headland at the end of the walk you can find the metal ground anchor of the old suspension bridge that spanned the lake during the enlargement works to the reservoir in the 1920s. Spare a thought for the poor architects as you cross Sheepstor Dam as its building caused them more headaches than that of the larger Burrator Dam and took over three years to construct.

Burrator Arboretum

This is a recently-constructed and planted tree garden, with bridges and a board walk next to the river, in a 40 acre area adjacent to the reservoir.

Starting point:	South of Norsworthy Bridge, with the car park on your left if you have come from Norsworthy Bridge.
Map reference:	568693
Distance:	As short or as far as you like
Terrain:	A lovely area to explore at will with an abundance of wildlife and trees which are already beginning to mature. You are surrounded by good moorland views. I would also recommend this to wheelchair users.

Checklist for pushchair alternatives

☐ A squirrel

☐ Tadpoles

☐ A fishing boat

☐ Canadian geese

☐ Butterflies

☐ A woodpecker

☐ Forget-me-Knots

☐ Flag irises

6. Cockington

Cockington is well worth a visit, particularly in Spring when the rhododendrons are out. It is best known for its village of thatched cottages which adorns many a souvenir or postcard from Devon. By doing this walk you will see that there is a lot more than at first meets the eye.

Starting point:	Torquay, South Devon. Cockington is signposted from Torquay town centre, or from the sea front, with the brown tourist signs. Park in the pay and display car parks in Cockington Village.
Car park map references:	893636 or 894639
Distance:	About 1½ miles
Terrain:	Good paths or country lanes, possible in all weathers. A few minor hills.
Maps:	OS Landranger 202, Torbay and South Dartmoor area. OS Pathfinder 1351, Torbay.
By bus:	During spring and summer there are mini-buses which leave the Princess Theatre every 20 minutes. Phone 01803 211467.
By horse and carriage:	From the sea front at Livermead. For further details phone 01803 607364.
Public Toilets:	Cockington Village, in the main car park (thatched toilets!). Cockington Court in the summer.
Refreshments:	Numerous cafés and The Drum Inn in Cockington village. Cockington Court in the summer.
Telephones:	Opposite the main car park in the village.
Pushchairs:	Possible for the whole route with just a few shallow steps to negotiate around the lakes.

1. Follow signposts from the village to Cockington Court.

☺ The village of Cockington is famous for its thatched cottages. Thatching was the traditional roofing method until the eighteenth century. Most labourers' cottages would have been built of cob (earth and straw) with thatched roofs from the local wheat reeds.

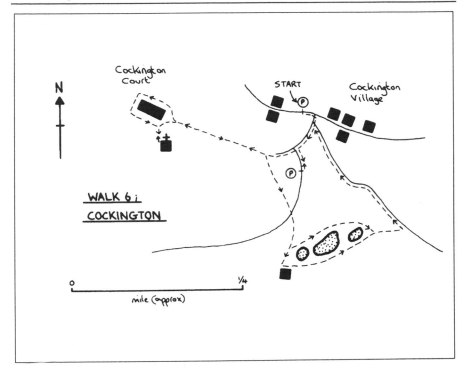

WALK 6 i
COCKINGTON

Today they are usually thatched from water reed from Eastern Europe, but with the ridges made from Devon wheat reed. The ridges tend to need replacing about every 7 years, whereas the actual roof can last for up to 60 years. Thatched roofs keep the houses warmer in winter and cooler in the summer.

There are now about fifty residents, whereas back in 1695 there were 360. It would be interesting to know how many tourists visit on a sunny summer's day! Originally the major industry of the village was fishing. Since 1946 the village has been owned by the Prudential Assurance Company.

Look out for the blacksmith's forge which, although it is a major tourist attraction, is still working. In the winter you can see horse shoes being made from molten metal and banged into shape on the anvil. There was once a pond in front of the forge where there was a ducking stool used as a punishment for minor crimes. The offender would have been bound to this device and ducked under the water.

The Drum Inn was designed by the famous architect Sir Edwin Lutyens and was opened in 1936. During the Second World War the Home Guard had their headquarters in its cellars!

2. **You will enter the
    parkland along the
    drive which ap-
    proaches Cockington
    Court. This is fre-
    quented by horses
    and carriages so you
    will have ample op-
    portunity for a lift in
    style if you wish, for
    a modest fee.**

☺ Note the bucket and
   shovels   hanging
   beneath the carriages
   — you won't find
   yourself   needing
   wellies on this walk.

The parkland is
beautiful with a wide
variety of trees and
lovely grass slopes,
with plenty of room
for running about or
for picnics.

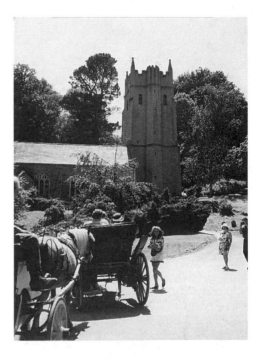

Cockington Church

Particularly in spring, there are lots of wild flowers such as
crocuses, snowdrops and daffodils. There are some wooden
benches to sit on. In front of Cockington Court is a cricket ground
with its pavilion above. In the summer, with the lush scenery and a
game of cricket playing, you could not be anywhere but in England.

☺ Cockington Court itself was originally a Saxon manor. It was built
   to its E-shaped plan in Tudor times by the Carey family, and was
   then given its eighteenth century facade by the Mallock family.

It now houses a craft centre as well as a tea room.

3. **Walk behind the house to the right to see some examples of
    rural crafts, and then through into the Rose Garden which is
    superb in the summer, both for its roses and their accompany-
    ing aroma, and for the climbing plants.**

☺ A variety of crafts are on display and you can sometimes see the craftsmen at work — for example, making wattle hurdles which were a traditional form of fencing.

4. **Go straight through the Rose Garden, out through the opposite gate and walk over to the Church of St George and St Mary.**

☺ The church is mostly 13th and 14th-century, built on Norman foundations, and is unusual in that it has no churchyard. The only graves are those of three beloved dogs owned by a gamekeeper in the early 1900s. Although the Church owns the building, it owns no land around it. At one point the owners of Cockington Court did not like visitors in the ground so locked the gates, but this meant that no one could reach the parish church. Eventually, the Church took the case to the High Court.

5. **Head back down the drive but just before you reach the end, bear to the right, signposted to the lakes. Turn right to the Gamekeeper's Cottage. You will pass a millstone before the path drops downhill through a dark tree-lined cutting and underneath the road bridge.**

☺ The Gamekeeper's Cottage was originally 16th-century, but was burned down by vandals in 1990. The last gamekeeper lived here in 1936. The building you now see is a reconstruction of the original, and it is possible to go in when it is open. It now houses an information centre about rural life and wildlife. Entry is free. The gamekeeper would have shared the lower floor with his pigs. The upper part of the building has a wooden-slatted gable used for hanging game. Upstairs you can see a thatched roof from inside. It reminds me of a fairy tale cottage. Look for the display of mantraps used to catch or deter poachers. Pheasant shooting became popular in the 19th century, and Cockington Estate employed a gamekeeper to look after these valuable birds. Nowadays no shooting is allowed so any pheasants you may see are free to roam here.

6. **Walk down the track below the Gamekeeper's Cottage, passing the lakes, and carry on downhill until you pass beneath the Lower Lodge and come to Cockington Lane.**

☺ The lakes are based on the ornamental ponds which are connected by a stream and were originally created in 1659.

Surrounding these ponds is very attractive woodland with a wide variety of ornamental trees such as rhododendrons, bamboo and hamamelis, just to name a few, giving the feel of an exotic jungle. Hamamelis is used to make witch hazel, which is an excellent treatment for bruises.

In the lakes you may see ducks and moorhens, and if you are lucky, perhaps a heron after a fish or two.

The Lower Lodge is a Gothic style gatehouse built of red sandstone and grit.

7. **Turn left along Cockington Lane and walk back into the village and to your car.**

☺ As you walk along the road, look at the pretty houses, and gardens with ponds and streams running through them.

Cockington is a very attractive village and therefore a honey pot for visitors in the summer, but out of season it will be a lot quieter. There are a number of gift shops selling souvenirs and crafts.

Checklist

☐ A thatched roof

☐ A mill stone

☐ An anvil

☐ A horse and cart

☐ A duck

☐ A fish

☐ A pheasant

☐ A moohen

7. Dartington

This walk takes you through beautiful woodland, parkland and farm land. It includes a visit to the renowned Cider Press Centre and the spectacular gardens at Dartington Hall. There are glorious views over the River Dart, and perhaps glimpses of a steam train making its way along the Dart Valley Railway, heralded by plumes of steam appearing through the trees.

Starting point:	Park in the free car park of Dartington Cider Press. The Cider Press can be reached on the Buckfastleigh to Totnes Road, near Shinner's Bridge.
Car park map reference:	788624
Distance:	About 3 miles
Terrain:	Good tracks and pavements. The track through the woods near the Cider Press Centre can get a bit muddy after heavy rain. There are a few hills, but nothing too taxing. There are steps to negotiate in the gardens of Dartington Hall.
Maps:	OS Landranger 202
By bus:	To Shinner's Bridge. For further details phone 01752 222666.
Public Toilets:	The Cider Press Centre and Dartington Hall, by the entrance.
Refreshments:	The Cider Press Centre sells snacks and meals, and also has picnic benches.
Pushchairs:	Possible for the whole route as long as you are prepared to negotiate steps in Dartington Hall Gardens.

1. **Head through the grounds of the Cider Press Centre towards Tridias Toy Shop.**

    The Cider Press Centre has an excellent range of shops, including Dartington Glass, a Cranks Restaurant, a delicatessen, a garden shop, a book shop and a very good toy shop called Tridias. The profits go towards a range of charitable activities, for example, to

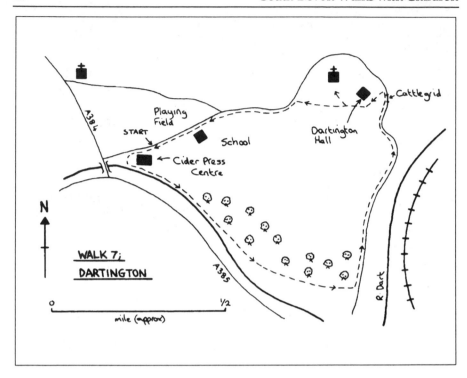

WALK 7;
DARTINGTON

enable Third World students to study. The telephone number is
01803 864171

☺ Cider is no longer manufactured here, but you can see the old
cider press near the car park and you can buy various local
ciders.

In the main holiday periods there is often free entertainment, for
example, jugglers.

☺ If you can tear yourselves away, the walk is well worth
continuing.

**2. The footpath is picked up just beside Tridias, next to the river
and running parallel to the A385 on its way to Totnes.**

☺ Look out for an old water mill and the leat which would have
supplied the mill.

3. **Pass some well-preserved lime kilns and a pottery seconds shop on your left. When the path forks, take the right fork to continue beside the river. There are some limestone quarries to your left. Keep going alongside the fields, which sometimes flood, until you reach the road.**

☺ There may be cattle or sheep on the fields, and perhaps ducks or Canadian geese when it's wet or flooded. Look out for a multitude of wild flowers throughout this walk including primroses, daffodils, violets, bluebells, wild garlic and strawberries.

4. **Turn left along the paved road and walk up the hill to Dartington Hall.**

☺ As you go up the hill you get wonderful views over the river and the Dart Valley. You may see swans, ducks and canoeists on the river, and on the other side you may catch glimpses of the steam train as it makes its way along the line from Buckfastleigh to Totnes. It is an idyllic scene — watching the cattle or sheep as they graze in these fields above the river, and perhaps the occasional squirrel and rabbit. I hear a rumour that there is something like a gazelle or an antelope!

5. **You now have two options: turn left over a cattle grid into Dartington Hall grounds and gardens, or alternatively, follow the road around. In both cases you will come out on the road to Foxhole.**

The public are normally granted access to the grounds of Dartington Hall provided there is no event taking place. The peaceful grounds must be treated with respect. A donation is invited to help with the upkeep.

Dartington Hall was bought in 1925 by Leonard and Dorothy Elmhirst. They restored the buildings and grounds and founded the school, and an international summer school. Leonard was a poet, a philosopher and a social reformer with an interest in farming, forestry and revitalising the countryside. Dorothy was passionate about the potential benefits of arts and crafts. Hence Dartington Hall is involved in a diversity of projects from the arts to agriculture. The estate is now managed by the Dartington Hall Trustees.

☺ Soak up the atmosphere of the lovely buildings in the quadrangle. Dartington Hall itself dates from 833, though most of the buildings you will see are more recent than this and have undergone sympathetic restoration after the Elmhirsts took over.

6. If you do choose to walk in the grounds, follow the path through the gardens and out through a wooden gate at the top. This will take you onto the road.

☺ You are in for a treat with the gardens which are very beautiful and stocked with a wide variety of plants, wild as well as exotic. Can you recognise any of these – magnolias, rhododendrons, daffodils, cyclamen, crocus, snowdrops or Christmas roses? The centre piece of the gardens is the tilt yard, once used for jousting and bear baiting. This is now used as an open air theatre with its raised grass terraces. There are various statues. Keep your eyes open for the squirrels leaping about as well as many small birds. You may notice part of a church behind the gardens. The rest of it was moved!

Dartington Hall Gardens

If you are gardeners, you may enjoy a look around the cottage garden shop which is well stocked with interesting plants.

7. Turn left out of the gate and walk down the hill on the pavement beside the road.

☺ As you drop down the hill towards Foxhole you have wonderful rural views and can see the intricate tower of Dartington Church in the distance.

8. Take the left turn towards Foxhole and follow the public footpath alongside playing fields until you reach the car parks of the Cider Press Centre.

☺ If you are lucky there may be a game of football or cricket being played.

Checklist

☐ Cider press

☐ Cows

☐ Swans

☐ Violets or primroses

☐ Donkey statue

☐ Rabbits

☐ Swan statue

☐ Squirrel

8. Dawlish

This is a superb walk with extensive coastal views and a backdrop of beautiful red sandstone cliffs. There will be plenty of opportunities to enjoy pottering on the beaches and to watch trains. The walk centres on Dawlish Town Centre with its shops and park, so it is worth taking some bread so that you can feed the birds. You could easily make a day of it with all there is to do in this area. Even in the winter, during a gale, it holds its attractions with dramatic waves.

Starting point:	If you can find a space, park in Marine Parade, which is free for 2 hours. Alternatively, there are a couple of car parks by the station, for which there is a charge.
Map reference:	Marine Parade: 963765
Distance:	Approx. 4 miles
Terrain:	Level paths, most of which are on the sea wall. Only one steep section at the beginning of the walk, but you will be rewarded by the views. After heavy seas there might be sand and shingle on the sea wall which could make it hard work with a pushchair. See note below.
Maps:	Landranger 192, Exeter, Sidmouth and surrounding area
By bus:	For further details phone 01803 613226, 01392 427711 or 01752 222666.
By train:	For further details phone 01345 484950.
Public Toilets:	By the lawn near the Tourist Information Bureau.
Telephones:	Near the Tourist Information Bureau and at the entrance to Marine Parade.
Refreshments:	All facilities in the town centre and a snack bar by the breakwater at Dawlish.
Pushchairs:	Possible for most of the walk unless there is too much debris on the sea wall from storms. There is a flight of steps about half way between Dawlish and Langstone Rock so this may be a good point to head back. **During rough weather you would need to use your discretion about walking on the sea wall as waves can crash over! Caution must always be exercised with young children when walking on the sea wall as there is quite a drop onto the beach or the sea, depending on the tide.**

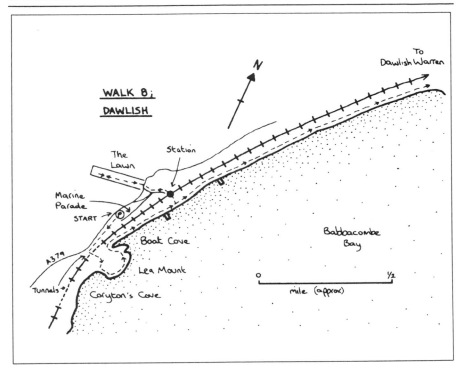

1. **Walk to the end of Marine Parade, with the railway line on your left. Follow the steep footpath up Lea Mount, and then before the path zigzags, drop down to Coryton's Cove. The superb views of the coastline, stretching as far as Portland Bill on a clear day, are well worth the effort.**

☺ There are amazing erosion formations in this stunning red sandstone cliff. It was once a sand dune. At the top there are some seats under cover where you can catch your breath while admiring the views.

Look to your right towards Teignmouth to see the fantastic sea stacks. These are called the Parson and the Clerk. Legend has it that in days gone by the Bishop of Exeter, who was a much loved and respected fellow, died in Dawlish. At the time of his death there was a wicked and greedy parson and his clerk who were delighted by his death as the parson wanted to take his place in the cathedral. Anyway, the devil turned them to stone when their horses leapt off the cliff in a storm, and they have remained there ever since.

Corytons Cove beach is a lovely place to play or to have a picnic.

2. **Head back towards Dawlish, passing through Boat Cove, and then joining the sea wall.**

Dawlish Breakwater

😊 At Boat Cove you can usually see boats, as its name suggests, often with people working on them. The beaches here and at Coryton's Cove are of red sand and shingle and in between are some very inviting rock pools. The beautiful sea stack is called Old Maid Rock, and is a resting place for seagulls.

The building with the turrets was once a gentlemen's club and was opened in 1895. Before this there were public baths offering hot or cold sea water baths. You should see a number of trains, and look out for the blackened tunnel near the footbridge at Boat Cove.

3. **You can now continue along the sea wall all the way to Langstone Rock and to Dawlish Warren beyond if you wish, before returning by the same route.**

☺ Dawlish Warren is a nature reserve with a wide variety of wildlife amongst its dunes. In contrast are all the traditional seaside entertainments and shops. I have not described this in any detail as you may want to visit it separately from this walk.

It is possible to walk along the breakwater at Dawlish in calm weather though take care at the end where there is slippery seaweed.

☺ Just beyond the breakwater you can see the railway station, which dates back to 1875. When the railway first came to Dawlish, it ran on a revolutionary system which was known as the Atmospheric Railway, designed by Brunel, which needed pumping houses every few miles to provide the right pressure in the rails. This system was not viable, although it was a great idea. The last complete pumping station is near Starcross.

4. **Once you get back to the Dawlish breakwater, you then go under the railway line, cross the road by the zebra crossing and head alongside Dawlish Water through the park.**

☺ Dawlish Water, or the Lawn as it is also known, is probably what people first think of when they think of Dawlish. It was once just swamp until it was laid out in 1808. Its most well-known residents these days are the black swans, which are of Australian origin. There is also a variety of ducks, moorhens, gulls and doves which like to be fed. Some of the birds are quite tame and will land on you for their feast! The park has lots of seats, some of which are under shelter and there is also a bandstand. At night this part of Dawlish Water, as it runs down to the sea over its little weirs, is lit with coloured lights. There is a pitch and putt course for those who fancy a go. At the other end of the park is a bowling green where you may be able to watch a match in progress.

There is a wide variety of shops and cafés nearby.

5. **Return to your car.**

Checklist

☐ Train

☐ Boat

☐ Fishermen

☐ Black swan

☐ Duck

☐ Shell

☐ Beach hut

☐ Bandstand

9. Exeter Canal Basin to Double Locks

This is a flat walk with a great variety of interest for all ages. You will be exploring some of the Exeter Ship Canal and the River Exe, crossing the bridges and lock gates and passing weirs. There is always plenty going on near the quay and Haven Banks with a variety of water sports, fishermen, cyclists, roller skaters and people feeding the birds, Ample opportunity to see wildlife, in particular herons, cormorants, swans, moorhens and ducks. In the summer there is a wealth of wild flowers, particularly along the river banks and canal.

Starting point:	Follow the signs to the Exeter Maritime Museum. (Unfortunately, at the time of writing this museum has closed.) Park in the Haven Banks car park (pay and display), or if there is space, in Haven Road, Isca Road, or Water Lane, which are free for up to 2 hours.
Car park map reference:	922915
Distance:	About 4 miles
Terrain:	Level paths of tarmac or gravel with very short stretches on grass.
Maps:	OS Landranger 192
By bus:	For further information phone 01803 613226 or 01392 427711.
By train:	For information phone 01345 484950.
Public Toilets:	At the quay
Refreshments:	Cafés, shops and two pubs on the quay. Café and shop at Haven Banks. The Malthouse pub in Haven Road with Charlie Chalks Fun Factory. Double Locks Inn has outside seating and serves food all day it also has a volleyball pitch and an assault course in its grounds. Port Royal Pub has outside seating.
Pushchairs:	Possible for the whole route, with only one point where it would need lifting. Double pushchairs or wheelchairs could manage the outward route to the Double Locks but would be advised to return by the same route to avoid the cycle prevention barriers on the other side of the river.

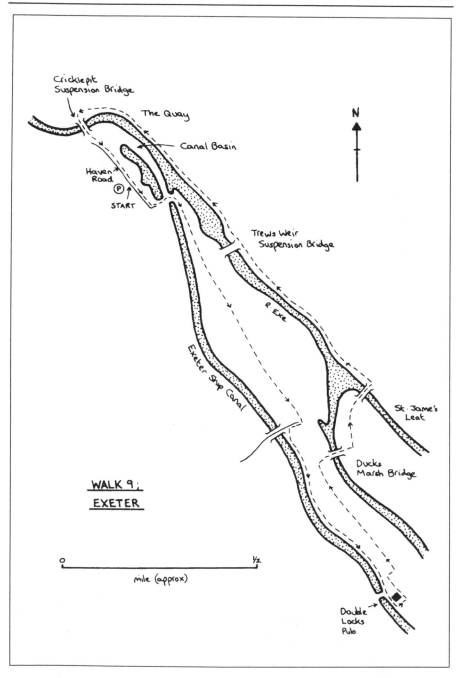

Cricklepit
Suspension Bridge

The Quay

Canal Basin

N

Haven
Road

START

Trews Weir
Suspension Bridge

R. Exe

Exeter Ship Canal

St. James's
Leat

Ducks
Marsh Bridge

WALK 9;
EXETER

0   ½

mile (approx)

Double
Locks
Pub

1. **Follow Haven Road past the canal basin.**

   You will pass a well-stocked chandler on your left, and then you will come to the canal basin with its variety of boats in and out of the water.

   ☺ The canal basin was constructed in 1830 and is 274 metres long and 30 metres deep.

2. **Cross the bridge over the canal basin. Turn right to walk beside the flood prevention channel.**

   ☺ There are often seagulls and cormorants sitting on the edge, and perhaps a heron may be fishing in the weir. In the past Exeter has suffered some dramatic floods.

3. **Follow the foot/cycle path across the plains as far as the huts by the playing fields. Here you have the choice of crossing the bridge to walk on the other side of the canal on the towpath, or walking alongside the canal on the pavement (the latter route is the same that the cars take). These paths take you to the Double Locks Inn.**

   ☺ If you chose to stay with the road, you will notice the tree trunks lining the roadside at regular intervals. These have been placed there as natural bollards to prevent people ditching their cars over the bank.

   Walking beside the canal, look out for moorhens, swans and ducks, not to mention canoeists. On the other side of the canal you will probably hear and see the trains rushing past. In the summer the canal is particularly attractive for its wild flowers, notably the Himalayan balsam and the yellow water lily. Watch out for the dramatic exploding seed capsules of the Himalayan balsam. The Himalayan balsam, which has pink flowers, was introduced to this country in 1839 and grown in greenhouses before it escaped into the wild. The yellow water lily is native to Britain, though you may well see it in water gardens as well as in the wild. It is also known as the "brandy bottle" due to the smell of stale alcohol from its flowers and also, the seed capsules bear a remarkable resemblance to tiny spirit bottles.

   The Exeter Ship Canal was built between 1564 and 1566 as far as the Countess Wear Bridge. It was the first lock canal to be built in Britain since Roman times. It was extended to the Turf Locks between 1820 and 1830. The canal was actually built to resolve a problem that lasted 300 years. The Countess of Devon had an argument with the people of Exeter about some salmon. She built a weir which stopped all the trading vessels getting upstream on the river to Exeter. Henry VIII gave permission for the canal to be built to by-pass this weir, which is no longer in existence.

The Double Locks Inn dates from 1701 and is thought to have been built by the Dutch. It was originally the lock keeper's house. Look for the old mounting blocks and the stables.

It is renowned for its breakfasts but serves a good range of food all day. There is an excellent assault course for children in the grounds and plenty of outside seating.

4. **On leaving the Double Locks Inn, head back towards Exeter. When you reach the second lock gates of the double lock, take the rough track a few steps to your right through a narrow gap in the fence to the field. Join the path heading towards Exeter.**

5. **Just before you reach the playing field pavilion, head a few yards across the grass to the right, through a kissing gate and over the Ducks Marsh Bridge.**

☺ This is the highest point at which the Exe is tidal. Upstream you will see the reason – St James's Weir.

6. **Cross the bridge over St James's Leat.**

Here you will come to a children's play area. Behind this is the College of Art and Design.

7. **Follow the footpath towards Exeter.**

☺ You will see the Trews Weir Suspension Bridge (built in 1935). Next you will come to Trews Weir itself, which was built in the 1560s by the engineer of the Exeter Ship Canal, John Trew, in order to create sufficient depth for the canal.

8. **Continue alongside the river to the quay.**

☺ You will pass the Port Royal Inn which was the scene of a freak tornado in September 1850!

Exeter Quay

Once you reach the quay you can see the old warehouses, mills and underground storage cellars. Some have been converted into apartments and offices, while others are used as antique and craft shops.

There is a shop called Saddles and Paddles where you can hire cycles or canoes. Tel: 01392 424241. You could also visit the Seahorse Nature Aquarium. Tel: 01392 438538. Boat trips can be booked. Tel: 01392 265700 or 265213.

9. **Return to your car via the wooden bridge and then the Cricklepit Suspension Bridge over the river. Alternatively, in the summer, for a nominal fee you could use the hand ferry.**

☺ This ferry has been in action since 1750, and is one of the only ferries of its kind in Europe. The wire is a hazard to unsuspecting mariners!

Checklist

☐ Canoe

☐ Water lily

☐ Cormerant

☐ Heron

☐ Duck

☐ Train

☐ Ferry Boat

☐ Jolly Roger flag pole

10. Teign Gorge from Fingle Bridge

This is an exceptionally dramatic walk, setting out from the picturesque Fingle Bridge and climbing up along the Hunter's Path, with its spectacular views of the wooded gorge and Castle Drogo. For further variety your return is by following the river back downstream along the Fisherman's Path.

Starting point:	Park near the Angler's Rest Pub at Fingle Bridge. It is one mile from Drewsteignton, which is signposted from the A30 and the A382. From Drewsteignton follow the signs to Fingle Bridge. If there are no spaces on this side of the bridge, cross over to the car park on the other side.
Car park map reference:	743899
Distance:	About 4 miles
Terrain:	Well-marked tracks, stony in places. Steep climb at the beginning of the walk but mostly level or downhill after this, except some steps on the Fisherman's Path.
Maps:	OS Landranger 191, Okehampton and North Dartmoor. OS Outdoor Leisure 28, Dartmoor.
By bus:	To Castle Drogo or Drewsteignton. For further details phone Barnstaple 45444, Beaworthy 221237, Cheriton Bishop 24333 or 01752 222666.
Public Toilets:	On the other side of Fingle Bridge from the Angler's Rest, at the far end of the car park.
Refreshments:	The Angler's Rest at Fingle Bridge and sweets and ice creams next door.
Pushchairs:	Not possible

1. From the Angler's Rest at Fingle Bridge, head down the road towards Drewsteignton until you see the Hunter's Path signpost on your left. Follow this track without turning off until you reach the road. This stretch is just over 1½ miles in length.

☺ Fingle Bridge, sometimes known as the bridge to nowhere, probably dates from about 1570 and seems rather narrow by modern standards, with recesses for pedestrians. It was actually designed for packhorses.

There was once a mill at Fingle Bridge, before it was destroyed by fire in 1894. You can find the remains downstream of the bridge, and also an inscription bearing the miller's name on a rock 50 yards upstream of the bridge with the date 1884. See if you can find it to see what his name was.

This is a very pleasant spot to spend time watching the river or perhaps to enjoy a drink and a meal in the Angler's Rest, which has outside seating in the summer.

☺ The first section of the Hunter's Path climbs steadily through the woodland over the Teign Gorge. There are many wood-ant hills here. Can you find any? Their industrious inhabitants are always on the move, carrying leaves or bits of wood far bigger than they are themselves. You may also spot squirrels, wild birds such as tree creepers, and birds of prey such as buzzards. If you are lucky you could see fallow deer.

The Teign Gorge

Your effort is soon to be rewarded with gorgeous views (excuse the pun!) of the heavily wooded Teign Gorge, with the dramatic Sharp Tor and Castle Drogo.

At Sharp Tor there is a path which heads uphill to Castle Drogo. It is well worth a detour to this surprisingly modern castle.

☺ Castle Drogo sits at this imposing site at the top of the Teign Gorge, at a height of 1000ft/300 metres above sea level. It was built by Sir Edwin Lutyens between 1910 and 1930 for Julius Drewe. Drewe had made his fortune in the grocery trade and gave Lutyens a budget of £60,000 with which to build the castle. It is now owned by the National Trust. Despite being a relatively modern building, it is very interesting to visit with fantastic views and a most ingenious bath and shower.

The National Trust welcomes children in this house and there is a special guide and questionnaire. For further details, telephone 01647 433306.

☺ The walk along the Hunter's Path is quite exhilarating, even in the wind and rain. The paths run between undergrowth of bracken, heather, gorse, brambles and sloes and honeysuckle. Look at how the spiders make good use of the gorse with their intricate and fine cobwebs. In the autumn this is a good walk to identify the different fungi. At strategic points you will find benches where you can take a rest and enjoy the views.

2. **At the road turn left and follow it until you reach the sign to Fingle Bridge on your left at Gib House, an attractive thatched cottage. Follow the footpath (Fisherman's Path) downstream with the river until you reach Fingle Bridge.**

☺ Shortly you will come to a metal bridge over the river. You can walk on this, though don't cross it for this walk. Downstream is a still pool of water which is where the salmon come to spawn in October. Downstream is a weir with a salmon leap. Further downstream still is a building which houses a turbine generator which supplies Castle Drogo with its electricity.

This walk along the Fisherman's Path is easy and very pretty. Where the path goes under Sharp Tor there are steps going up and over the rock face.

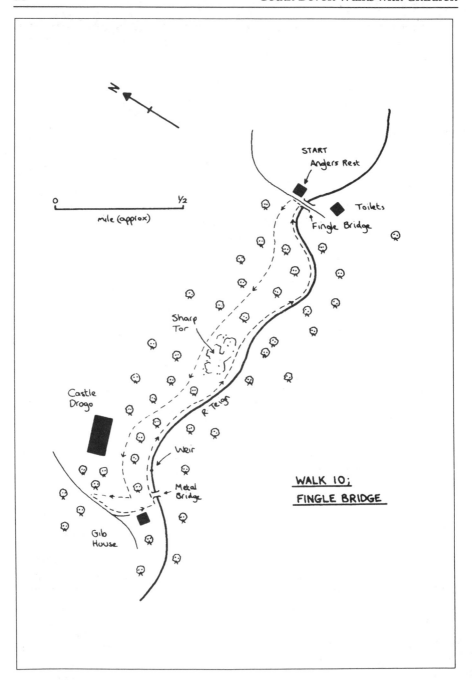

N

0   ½
mile (approx)

START
Anglers Rest

Toilets

Fingle Bridge

Sharp
Tor

Castle
Drago

R Teign

Weir

Metal
Bridge

Gib
House

WALK 10;
FINGLE BRIDGE

Every so often you will see slopes of rubble. This area is in the metamorphic aureole which surrounds Dartmoor. It tends to have a width of about a mile. This sedimentary rock, much older than granite, was cooked and contorted when the molten lava (now the granite of Dartmoor) was forced up by volcanic upheaval. The River Teign then cut through these comparatively soft rocks to form the gorge. The rocks include slate and sandstone.

These woods have been used for forestry purposes but the remaining oak woodland is now protected. The area covered in this walk is now owned by the National Trust so should remain unspoiled for all of us to enjoy for many years to come.

Checklist

☐ Ant hill

☐ Fisherman

☐ Spiders web

☐ Robin

☐ Deer

☐ Squirrel

☐ Rabbit

☐ Acorn

11. Haldon Hill

This is an adventurous exploration of the forest, where you can let
your imagination run riot. There is fun for all ages with a tunnel,
stepping stones, logs to clamber over and streams to paddle in as well
as lots of wildlife to spot and identify.

Starting point:	Bird of Prey car park on Haldon Hill. From the A38, travelling in the Exeter direction, take the slip road opposite the racecourse towards Dunchideock. Follow the brown Forestry Commission signs. The Bird of Prey car park is on your left after the Bullers Hill car park.
Car park map reference:	876855
Distance:	Up to 1½ miles
Terrain:	Rough tracks, could be muddy. Some slopes, but of no great difficulty. Take wellies in wet weather or if the children cannot resist paddling.
Maps:	OS Landranger 192, Exeter, Sidmouth and surrounding area. OS Pathfinder 1329, Topsham and Doddiscombleigh.
By bus:	No
Public Toilets:	None
Refreshments:	None, take a picnic.
Pushchairs:	Not suitable for this route. Alternative at the end of this walk.

1. **Go through wooden posts marked Bird of Prey. Take the path
    immediately to your left marked with a small post with a
    butterfly. The path takes you downhill.**

    If you wish, before starting the walk, go straight on through the
    posts to the Bird Of Prey View Point. Here are attractive wooden
    benches where you can enjoy the panoramic views over the Teign
    Valley and the moors.

    ☺ See if you can spot some birds of prey. In the summer there are
    some leaflets supplied at the posts by the car park which will help
    you identify the birds of prey. It is possible that you could see

Birds of Prey Viewpoint

common buzzards, honey buzzards, sparrow-hawks, goshawks, hobbies, kestrels, peregrines, red kites or ospreys.

Binoculars would be useful.

2. **Go through the gap in the fence and turn right at another butterfly sign. The path goes downhill.**

☺ There are many trees here for you to identify including conifers, silver birch, beech, oak, sycamore and rowan. Wild flowers include heather, whortleberries and orchids. Particularly in the autumn, there are many varieties of fungi to identify, but **do not touch as many are poisonous**.

3. **At the bottom of the hill turn right, following signs to the Butterfly Walk. You will notice some marker posts with red and green paint. This is a wide forestry track and mostly level.**

4. **At the second post, turn left.**

☺ You will pass a bench on your right and a log on your left – great for playing on. Next you will come to a wishing well and then an overturned tree trunk (or is it a giant spider's web?). A little

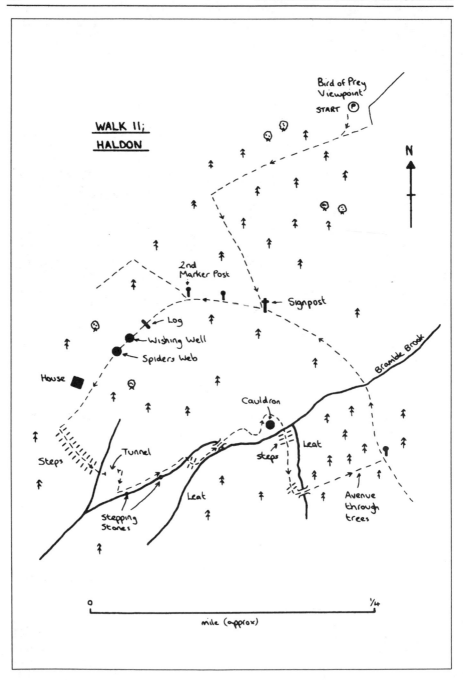

WALK 11;
HALDON

Bird of Prey
Viewpoint
START

N

2nd
Marker Post

Signpost

Log
Wishing Well
Spiders Web

House

Bramble Brook

Cauldron

Steps

Tunnel

Leat

Steps

Leat

Stepping
Stones

Avenue
through
trees

0   ¼

mile (approx)

further on you will reach a charming little house, straight out of a fairy tale book with a working fire place. **(Great caution must always be exercised when lighting fires in woods, particularly in the summer when one stray spark could set the woods alight.)**

The "house" to be found on this walk

5. There is a shallow wooden step opposite the entrance to the house. Step down here and head down the slope, slightly to the right for about 50 metres to a flight of wood-edged steps. Go down these and cross the wooden bridge.

6. Head down to your right, and on your left you will see a tunnel. Go through the tunnel.

7. Cross the stepping stones on your left and go along the wooden walkway, through the little gorge. Go up the slope to the bench and then on to the track behind, going to the right for a few yards until you see a pond on your right.

☺ The stepping stones and the walkway are all made of wood and are a most attractive feature out in this wilderness.

8. **Go down to the pond and traverse it by the stepping stones. Go through the wooden arch and up some steps to the main path, next to the leat.**

9. **Turn left and follow the leat upstream. Cross the brook and go up the slope.**

☺ You will see a wooden cauldron on your right. Perhaps you might like to try your hand at making a potion. Bubble, bubble, toil and trouble!

10. **Turn right by the cauldron. Cross the stream on the stepping stones and climb up the steps.**

11. **Follow the path until you come to some steps on your left which take you through an earth bank and over a small footbridge. Next go through the avenue through the dark yet beautiful woods straight ahead.**

12. **When you reach the main track with the red and green marker post, turn left.**

13. **Turn right up the track signposted 'Bird of Prey'. When you come to the fence with the gap, go through it and back to your car.**
    At the signpost, if you were to go straight ahead, you would reach the Butterfly Walk. There are 34 species of butterflies which breed in the forest.

Checklist

☐ Butterfly

☐ Bird of prey

☐ Orchid

☐ Whortleberry

☐ Pinecone

☐ Flint

☐ Sycamore leaf or seed

Pushchair Route: Mamhead

This is an easy, short walk with spectacular views from the other side of the Haldon Hill ridge.

Starting point:	Mamhead Forest Walks Car Park. From the A380 take the road to Mamhead. About half a mile along this road, turn right at a sign to the "Old Stable". The car park is in about half a mile on your left.
Car park map reference:	922805
Distance:	Less than 1 mile
Terrain:	Good, level tracks suitable for wheelchairs and even double pushchairs.
Maps:	OS Landranger 192
Toilets:	None
Refreshments:	None. Picnic benches at the Obelisk.

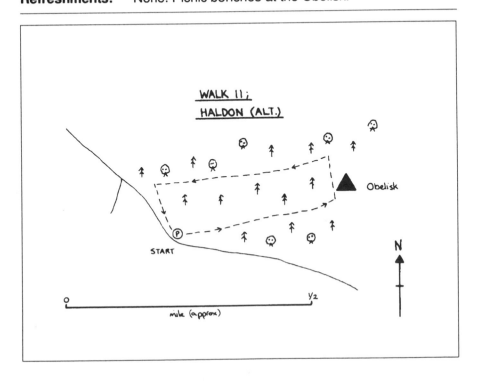

Follow the yellow waymarked route for wheelchair users to take in the Obelisk and Tebbits Copse. This circuit can be done in either direction.

☺ This walk takes you through mixed woodland and heathland. The Obelisk is a superb vantage point from where you have a bird's eye view over the Exe Estuary and out to sea, on a clear day as far as Sidmouth and Lyme Regis, and over the fields and trees and Mamhead House. The Obelisk is built of Portland stone and is 100ft/30m high. It was built by Thomas Balle in 1743 as a guide to mariners.

Mamhead House was garrisoned by the Royalists in the Civil War. It has been rebuilt twice since then.

Tebbits Copse was opened by Lady Tebbit in 1993 as a wheelchair route. At the same time trees were planted by local children. Look out for birds and squirrels. In August the heather and gorse is spectacular, and you may be able to pick whortleberries and blackberries.

12. Haytor

This is a most impressive, exhilarating walk taking in Dartmoor's best known tor, and the picturesque Haytor Quarries. The views from Haytor are spectacular – taking in Dartmoor and the surrounding countryside and right out to sea. On a clear day you can see from Portland Bill to Start Point, with the Teign Estuary clearly visible on reasonably fine days.

Starting point:	Park in the Haytor Rocks car park opposite the Tor. The car park is free, quite large and often has an ice cream van.
Car park map reference:	759768
Distance:	Approx. 1¼ miles
Terrain:	Rough tracks, not very clearly defined in places. Medium gradients. Haytor can be windy, so go prepared. Do not attempt this walk in poor visibility unless you are confident with a map and compass, as **there are no signposts**.
Maps:	1:25 000 Outdoor Leisure Map 28, side b
By bus:	For further details phone 01803 613226 or 01752 222666.
Public Toilets:	At the Haytor Vale car park, a short distance down the road in the direction of Bovey Tracey.
Refreshments:	Usually there are ice cream or snack vans at the Haytor car park and the Haytor Vale car park.
Pushchairs:	Possible as long as you are feeling fairly energetic and are prepared to manoeuvre around rocks and perhaps drag the pushchair backwards in places.

1. **From the car park, head north up to Haytor itself. There are a number of worn tracks – it is better to keep to these so as not to add to the erosion.**

☺ The views are terrific, looking out to sea and to surrounding tors such as Hound Tor, Rippon Tor and the aptly named Saddle Tor, to name just a few. To the east you are looking towards Lustleigh Cleave and the Haldon Hills near Exeter.

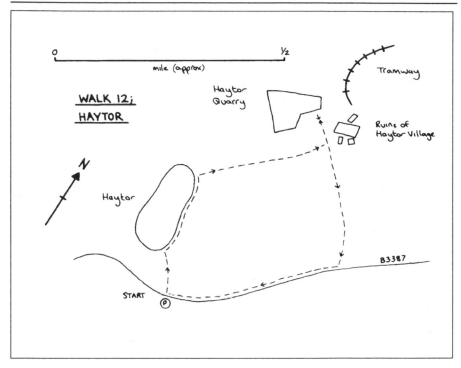

😊 Haytor, or Heytor Rocks as it was once known, stands at about 1491ft/454metres above sea level. Its name is thought to mean "High Tor". To many, Haytor is the symbol of Dartmoor. If you fancy climbing to the top this is a fairly easy scramble as there are rough-hewn steps cut out in the rock to assist you.

Of course, great caution must be exercised due to the heights involved. On windy days the climb would not be safe for younger children.

If you don't want to reach the peak yourself, you can watch the antics of the climbers doing it the hard way, or perhaps see them abseiling back down.

To the left of Haytor itself (as you face it from the road) is Low Man. There are some iron railings to assist. It is said that these were put in place for Queen Victoria. The cliff off Low Man is roughly 40 metres/120ft high and is said to be the greatest natural rock face on Dartmoor.

2. Head east around Haytor Rocks until you pick up a barely discernible path which heads northeast, downhill to Haytor Quarries. The quarries are fenced and you will find a gate at the end of the well-defined track coming from the road.

☺ Quarrying for granite started here in 1820. Prior to this, surface granite was sufficient for local needs. The quarry was owned by George Templer, who built a tramway linking Haytor Quarries to the Stover Canal. This is now known as the Templer Way and is

Haytor quarry

another good walk. The track was just over 8 miles long with granite rails, and the wagons were horse-drawn. Part of London Bridge was built with rock from Haytor Quarries. The last work was in 1919 for a war memorial in Exeter. You can still see some of the winding and lifting gear.

The lakes are a very pleasant spot for a picnic as they are relatively sheltered. Watch out for birds, dragonflies and rabbits. You may see some goldfish amongst the water lilies. This area is unrivalled for its whortleberries. These are a type of blueberry which ripen in August and are delicious made into pies, jam or muffins, although the picking is a labour of love on these low-lying bushes as the berries are tiny and hidden. It was once an annual tradition for the locals to go out picking whortleberries together, taking picnics. There would have been a holiday atmosphere and later many of the berries would have been sold in the local markets.

3. **Leave the quarry through the gate you entered by and follow the track to the road. Walk on the grass beside the road back to the car.**

☺ You will probably come across Dartmoor ponies and their smaller counterparts, the imported Shetland ponies, some sheep and perhaps cattle. The most common breed of sheep is the hardy Scottish Blackface. It is usual for them to lamb in March or April, after the worst of the winter. For most of the year the ponies are left to their own devices until the round-up "drifts" in October when they are collected together, identified according to their farmer's brand, and then sorted and either released back on to the moor or taken to market.

As you leave the quarry, if you veer to the left towards a pair of weathered larch trees, you will come upon the ruins of the village built by George Templer for the quarry workers and their families. There is said to have been a school and a pub here. It is amazing that there is so little to be seen.

Checklist

☐ Climber

☐ Sheep

☐ Shetland pony

☐ Newts

☐ Heather

☐ Whotleberries or their plants

☐ Water lilies

☐ Adder

13. Hound Tor

This is Dartmoor at its most dramatic with gigantic pillars of rock and views for miles around at Hound Tor, followed by an exploration of a medieval village. Later you will cross a little clapper bridge and climb up to Smallacombe Rocks and on to the impressive Holwell Quarries under Haytor.

Starting point:	Free car park at Swallerton Gate. This is reached from the Haytor to Widecombe road. Take the turning to the right towards Manaton, Moretonhampstead and Chagford. You will see Hound Tor before you reach the car park.
Car park map reference:	739792
Distance:	About 3½ miles
Terrain:	Grass tracks or narrow dirt tracks which can be muddy or a bit slippery if wet. One set of stepping stones to negotiate. Hilly, but well worth the effort!
Maps:	OS Landranger 191, Okehampton and North Dartmoor area
Public Toilets:	None
Refreshments:	Ice cream van which also sells hot snacks at popular times.
Pushchairs:	Not suitable

1. From the car park walk directly ahead of you up Hound Tor.

☺ The remote house at Swallerton Gate was once a cider house or inn in the days of wool prosperity on the moor.

Hound Tor is tremendously spectacular with its pillars of rock towering over you from all angles. This is a great place to explore and scramble over. From the rocks you get good views towards Manaton, Chinkwell and Honeybag Tors, Haytor, Grea Tor, and Smallacombe Rocks.

There are a number of reports of ghostly black hounds on Hound Tor. The dogs have supposedly been spotted as recently as 1965. Reverend Baring-Gould claimed that the tor's name came

Hound Tor

about because the rock formations look like the heads of dogs. Whenever I have visited, all I have seen are grazing cattle, sheep and ponies. This is also a good spot to watch climbers as they climb and abseil on these rock faces.

Granite is a rock which although physically strong, is actually chemically weak. A combination of acid rain and acids from the peaty soil have acted on the felspar crystals turning them into kaolin or clay. Also, the joints in the rock were opened up during the ice age 10,000 years ago, levering the blocks apart. Some of them fell, so creating the clitter on the sides of some of the tors.

2. Go over the top of Hound Tor and down the hill, slightly to your right, in the direction of the remains of the medieval village. You follow quite a wide grassy track.

☺ This must have been a glorious setting for a village. The remains which you can see date from before the Norman Conquest, but there are remains dating much earlier. This area was excavated in 1961. There are about eleven houses, which would have been built of wattle and turf. The first building you come to is actually a barn with corn drying ovens at one end. In the 13th century the climate deteriorated so that this subsistence farming was

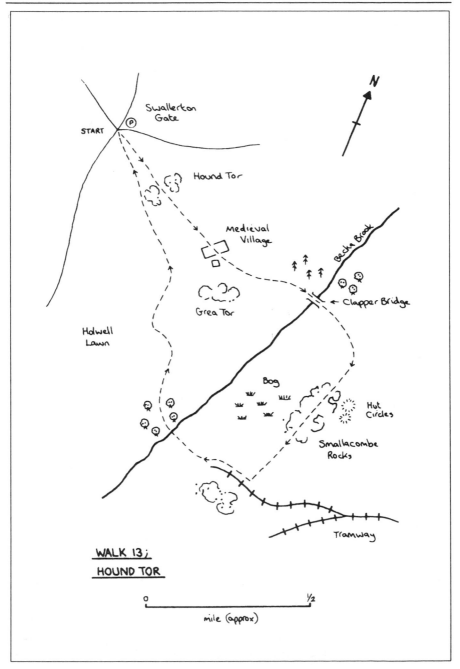

Swallerton Gate

START

Hound Tor

Medieval Village

Backa Brook

Clapper Bridge

Grea Tor

Holwell Lawn

Bog

Hut Circles

Smallacombe Rocks

Tramway

N

WALK 13;
HOUND TOR

0   ½

mile (approx)

threatened. The only way they could keep going was to dry the corn to store it over the winter. From Grea Tor, once the bracken has died back, you can make out the ancient field systems.

At the time of the Domesday Book, in 1086, the Hound Tor village was owned by Tavistock Abbey. There were about twenty people, seven cattle, twenty-eight sheep and eighteen goats. The villagers would have used berries and hunted game to supplement what they cultivated. The houses would have housed the animals next to the people. It is likely that this village may have been emptied during the Black Death in 1348.

3. **From the village, follow the path to the top edge of the woods to your left (having detoured up Grea Tor which reaches a height of 365 metres/1,200ft above sea level, if you wish). Go through the gate and follow the bridle path signposted to Leighon via Haytor Down. This path takes you downhill, through a couple more latch gates, until you cross the Becka Brook by the clapper bridge. TAKE THIS TRACK CAREFULLY AS IT IS FAIRLY STEEP AND MAY BE A LITTLE SLIPPERY. Every so often you will come across granite strips which have been placed to slow down the erosion, both by water and feet.**

☺ In the summer you will find bracken towering above you. You will walk beside a forest of larch trees. These are very attractive trees, being deciduous the needles change colour in the autumn before dropping. The cones hang onto the branches long after the needles have dropped. They provide a durable timber which is used for fence posts and cladding.

The clapper bridge and its surrounding area is charmingly peaceful. It is a few miles upstream from the well known Becky Falls.

4. **Follow the path straight on from the bridge. At the signpost head straight up the hill and follow the track when it veers to the right up to Smallacombe Rocks.**

☺ In the woods look out for squirrels and birds. There are hazel, rowan, birch and oak, crab apple trees, honeysuckle, foxgloves, fungi and whortleberries for you to identify.

The views from Smallacombe are superb, and this is a wonderful place to enjoy just sitting or scrambling over the rocks. The area around the rock is flat and you may well be joined by ponies who have come for a good scratch on the rocks, or to find any obliging walker who can help them relieve their itches! Please note that you must not feed them, whatever they might be saying, as by encouraging them to rely on people for food, you will be encouraging them to congregate on the roads where they could be hit by cars.

There are some fine hut circles near the rocks. These were probably Bronze Age and would have had conical roofs of turf or thatch. Some huts were for people to live in, some were for storage and cooking, and others were to shelter the livestock. In late summer the heather and gorse here make a spectacular display.

If your back can stand it, this is quite a good spot for picking the whortleberries.

5. **Go over the top of Smallacombe Rocks and take the path towards Holwell Quarries.**

☺ This is a superb stretch of easy, downhill walking with fantastic views. Below you, notice the hillside bog with its different plants such as the scabious and the cotton grass. Each of the white hairs of the cotton grass is attached to a seed. This enables the seed to be carried to a new location by the wind. The bright green moss is sphagnum moss which forms the notorious feather bed bogs which wobble when you walk on them. I do not advise this as the moss forms a blanket over water and mud. Sphagnum moss was used in the 1st World War as a wound dressing to staunch blood flow. It was also often used as an early form of disposable nappy! See how many different types of heather you can identify in the late summer.

6. **When you reach the tramway, turn right and continue along it, passing the rock faces of the quarry.**

☺ The granite tramway was used between about 1825 and 1858. The stone was loaded on to wooden-wheeled trucks which were pulled by teams of horses to Teigngrace, the head of the Stover Canal, where the stone was transferred to barges to go down the River Teign and to their destination by sea. The tramways run for about eight and a half miles and fortunately for the horses, much of the journey was downhill, aided by a primitive braking system. The use of the granite for rails was the innovative idea of the quarry owner, George Templer, to save money by using the readily available granite instead of the expensive iron rails. To cope with the upward slope from Holwell Quarry, the wagons were drawn by teams of up to nineteen horses. Twelve wagons, each bearing 35 tons, were taken up each time.

Rock from these quarries has been shipped to various destinations, including London to be used in the building of London Bridge and the British Museum. Near the rock face of the quarry you can see the ruins of a building which was probably the blacksmith's shop. Just below the tramway on your right is a platform with an unusual building, sometimes known as the Beehive Hut, which was actually a shelter for quarrymen where they could take refuge during blasting.

The rocks were split into manageable pieces by drilling holes of about 4 inches deep at regular intervals, and then wedges were put in each hole. Each wedge would then be tapped in sequence until the rock split, hopefully in the required direction. This must have been very hard work in those days without all our modern tools!

7. **At the end of the track, take the track down the hill to your right. It goes through a gap in the rowan trees and down to a stream which you cross by stepping stones. Follow the track up the hill and through the gate, where there is a sign to Hound Tor and Bonehill across Holwell Lawn. There is a map here.**

☺ Rowan berries can be used to make a tart-tasting jelly to accompany meat. Birds like these berries and as the berries pass through their digestive systems the seeds are distributed, often to remote crags.

This part of the river is a lovely spot to stop for a rest or perhaps a picnic. Look out for fish in the river.

8. **At the next signpost take the right turning for Hound Tor Down. Veer to your left when you reach the wire fence. You can now see Grea Tor ahead of you.**

☺ This area is sometimes used for horse jumping events. Look out for birds — the green woodpecker, for example.

9. **Go through the gate and along the middle grassy track up to Hound Tor, leaving Grea Tor to your right and then behind you.**

☺ If you notice burnt gorse and heather, this is probably as a result of swaling, where the heathland is burnt on purpose. Heather can live for up to thirty years. If a whole heather sward were to live to old age and then die, the entire sward would disappear at one time. Regeneration would be slow and other plants might take over, so the heather could disappear. There is also a problem if the heather is burnt when it is old and leggy as the resulting heat of the fire may be so great that the roots themselves, along with the seeds, would be killed. Therefore the people of Dartmoor try to work together so that swards of heather at different ages exist. This is good for wildlife as well as the grazing farm animals, and also explains why the best displays of flowering heather change in location from one year to another.

Common gorse flowers all year round, hence the saying, "When gorse is not in flower, kissing's gone out of fashion."

10. From Hound Tor go down the hill to the car park.

About 800 metres along the road to Chagford is Jay's Grave, always with fresh flowers on it. Who leaves the flowers is a mystery. The tragic is that Kitty Jay, a young local girl, fell in love with a local boy and was sure that they were to marry. The young man then spurned her and poor Kitty committed suicide. As was the custom in those days, she was buried without ceremony at the crossroads so that her soul would not know which way to haunt.

Checklist

☐ Cow

☐ Dartmoor pony

☐ Larch cone

☐ Medieval oven

☐ Hut circle

☐ Clapper bridge

☐ Beehive hut

☐ Tramway

14. Kenton, Powderham and Turf Inn

If you are keen on birdwatching, train spotting, boats, castles and herds of deer then this is the walk for you. The walk starts in the picturesque village of Kenton, takes you through lush countryside beside Powderham Castle and along the Exe Estuary to the Turf Inn. Although the return is by the same route, there is so much to see that you will find you notice new things on your return journey. I would recommend you take binoculars with you on this walk for deer and bird spotting in particular.

Starting point:	Park in the free car park in Kenton near the village green. Kenton is on the A379 between Exminster and Starcross.
Car park map reference:	959833
Distance:	About 5 miles
Terrain:	Paths and a short stretch on a minor road. Some of the paths can be muddy. Mostly flat with one easy hill.
Maps:	OS Landranger 192, Exeter, Sidmouth and surrounding area
By bus:	To Kenton. For further details phone 01803 613226 or 01392 427711.
Public Toilets:	In Starcross (not on the route) and in Turf Inn (if open).
Telephone Box:	In Kenton car park
Refreshments:	Turf Inn, with outside seating and play area for children. Pubs and shops in Kenton.
Telephone numbers:	Turf Hotel 01392 832843. Powderham Castle 01626 890729.
Pushchairs:	Not recommended, but possible with two adults and a narrow wheel-based pushchair.

1. **From the car park, cross the main road opposite the green and take the public footpath. This path takes you alongside a canalised river out of Kenton, between some marshy fields and the parkland of Powderham Castle.**

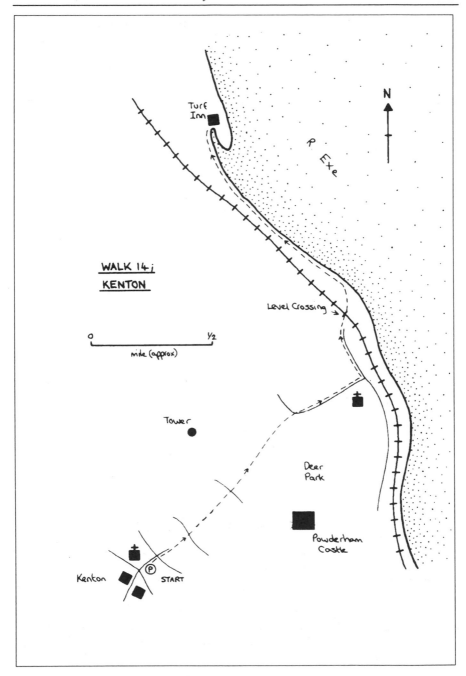

N

Turf
Inn

R Exe

WALK 14j
KENTON

0   ½
mile (approx)

Level Crossing

Tower

Deer
Park

Powderham
Castle

Kenton

START

☺ Kenton is very pretty, particularly in the summer with its window boxes. Do visit the old-fashioned stores by the post office. It is hard to believe that ships once sailed as far as Kenton, and in the 16th century cargoes of salt left for La Rochelle and returned with French wines and spirits. In 1856 Kenton was half destroyed by fire as most of the buildings were of cob and thatch. One of its inhabitants, Stanley Lake, invented traffic signals, the forerunners of our traffic lights. In the Second World War a German pilot was captured after he parachuted down into the High Street.

The footpath follows a river with some willow trees on the other bank. It comes out of the village with picturesque fields and marsh land on your left. You may think that you can see bulrushes here. These are, in fact, reedmaces. The confusion arises because of the Victorian painting called *Moses in the Bulrushes* which actually shows a cradle in a clump of reedmaces. These are much more spectacular than the bulrushes.

On your right you get your first glimpses of the grounds of Powderham Castle and you will soon see the roof of the castle. The name "Powderham" is derived from "Polder" meaning reclaimed land. Ahead of you is a pretty, red-brick house.

2. **Cross the narrow footbridge. Shortly you will come to a road which crosses the path. Ignore this and continue on the footpath up the hill.**

☺ When you cross the bridge, have a look in the river to see if you can spot some fish hiding in the weeds. As you climb the hill you have superb views over Powderham and its deer park, where you should spot many deer. Binoculars may help you unless you are lucky to have some deer close to you. These are fallow deer.

Powderham is the historic family home of the Earl of Devon and is open between April and October for guided tours. It was built between 1390 and 1420, but was badly damaged in the Civil War, so a great deal of renovation and alterations have taken place in the 18th and 19th centuries. Notice the beautiful, gnarled tree trunks.

3. **At the crest of the hill, cross the stile and follow the track along the edge of the field with the hedge on your left. Go through the gate at the bottom. Ahead of you are two thatched cottages.**

Powderham

☺ As you enter the field look up to your left to see Powderham Belvedere, the red brick tower built in 1773. Ahead and below you are superb views over the parkland and across the Exe Estuary.

4. **Follow the road to your right, passing one of the entrances to Powderham Castle, and walk down the road to Powderham Church.**

☺ Apparently cannon balls have been dug out of a tree by Powderham Church!

5. **Follow the footpath towards the Turf Hotel. After about 5 minutes cross the railway line, taking great care. Continue along the path beside the Exe Estuary until you reach the Turf Inn.**

6. **Return the way you came.**

☺ The Exe Estuary is a renowned place for birdwatching, particularly for waders. There are frequent trains passing on the railway line. On the other side of the estuary is Lympstone Commando Station where Prince Edward did his training.

In the summer the Turf Inn is a lovely place to stop and have lunch or refreshments outside, near the canal.

☺ You may see various river craft which have made their way down from Exeter.

It is possible to walk beside the canal to reach the Double Locks Inn described in another of these walks.

Weather and tide permitting, there are plenty of boats to watch on the estuary.

Checklist

☐ Train

☐ Thatched cottages

☐ Deer

☐ Castle

☐ Boat

☐ Oyster catcher

☐ Church

☐ Lock gates

15. Dartmouth from Kingswear

This walk starts and finishes in Kingswear so you will have the added fun of the upper and lower ferries. As you approach Dartmouth from Kingswear you get excellent views of Dartmouth and the Naval College. You will head out to the castle, with its beautiful views of the estuary and Kingswear, before returning to explore some of Dartmouth itself. As well as the fabulous views on this walk your other senses will be assailed with the smell of the sea and the sounds of the boats and steam trains.

Starting point:	Kingswear. Park in the Darthaven Marina car park (for a fee in the summer, but free in the winter). To get to this car park follow signs to the Lower Ferry and turn off to the right, following the car park signs, just before you reach the ferry.
Car park map reference:	884513
Distance:	About 3½ miles
Terrain:	Mostly pavement or track suitable for all weathers. The stretch out to Dartmouth castle is a bit hilly but well worth it for the views.
Maps:	OS Landranger 202 and OS Outdoor Leisure 20, South Devon
By bus:	To Kingswear. For further details phone 01803 613226 or 01752 222666.
Public Toilets:	Kingswear – in the Square, opposite the station. Dartmouth – by the Royal Avenue Gardens. Dartmouth Castle.
Refreshments:	Numerous cafés and restaurants in Dartmouth. Dartmouth has a full range of shops. There are a number of small shops on your way to the Lower Ferry in Kingswear.
Telephones:	By the Royal Avenue Gardens
Pushchairs:	Possible for the whole route, with the exception of going around Dartmouth Castle as it was not designed with this in mind! A double buggy would be feasible if you miss out the last stretch of the walk and return by the Lower Ferry.

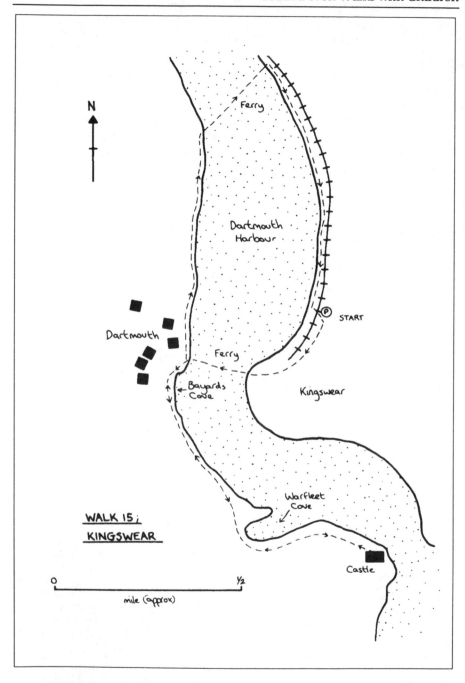

N

Ferry

Dartmouth
Harbour

Dartmouth

START

Ferry

Kingswear

Bayards
Cove

Warfleet
Cove

**WALK 15;
KINGSWEAR**

Castle

0   ½

mile (approx)

1. **Turn right out of the car park and follow the road around to the station and the ferry. Cross the river on the Lower Ferry which charges a small fee. The ferry crosses to and fro all day but there may be queues in the summer.**

☺ This small car ferry is unusual as it is actually a raft which is pushed across the river by a tug. From the ferry you can enjoy the views of Dartmouth, which is dominated by the Britannia Royal Naval College, built in 1902-5 by Sir Aston Webb, appropriately on the same site where the Raleigh family once lived. Before it was built, the naval college was housed in a couple of warship hulks moored on the river which were far from ideal as disease kept on breaking out owing to such large numbers of cadets living in close quarters.

Attractive houses line the narrow streets as they climb the hills above this deep water harbour. Dartmouth became important commercially in the 14th century with the growth of the wine trade with south-west France, and also Devon's cloth trade. One of the

Dartmouth

medieval merchants, John Hawley, was probably the inspiration for the Shipman in Chaucer's *Canterbury Tales*. Following a decline in the late Middle Ages, there was a revival of prosperity between 1580 and 1643 with the development of the fishing trade with Newfoundland and a revival of the cloth trade.

During the Second World War Dartmouth was very much involved in the preparations for the D-Day landings and on 6th June 1944, 480 assault and support craft left the harbour to join the rest of the armada in the channel. Kingswear had its part to play as General de Gaulle had his headquarters there. These days there is always plenty of activity out on the water to watch.

2. **Once you reach Dartmouth, follow signs to the castle. Walk along South Street, turn left at Warfleet Bridge, then left at the next fork to Dartmouth Castle.**

It is possible to catch a ferry out to Dartmouth Castle in the summer, so if you prefer this option, walk into Dartmouth and you will find the ferry leaves from the Embankment opposite Dartmouth Hospital.

☺ The walk out to Dartmouth Castle is a little hilly but is well worth the effort for the superb views back over Dartmouth and over the estuary to Kingswear. It is fun to look at the houses with their enviable views and imagine who must live in them. Warfleet Creek is an ancient anchorage used in the time of the Armada.

Dartmouth Castle is 14th-century, but with later modifications. Henry the 8th had cannons added and ordered a chain to be stretched across the river to Kingswear Castle at night to defend the town. This later became known as "Jawbones". During the Civil War Dartmouth was for the King. In 1646 the Parliamentary troops took the town by surprise just before midnight. Only Kingswear Castle held out and the two castles are said to have fired cannon balls at each other for weeks. Dartmouth Castle was also used in the Second World War. Despite its colourful history, it is in a remarkably good state of repair.

Dartmouth Castle is open all year. For further details telephone 01803 833588.

Next to the castle is St Petrox Church.

3. **Return to Dartmouth the way you came and explore the town.**

☺ Just before you reach the slip for the Lower Ferry is Bayards Cove with its castle which was built in 1510. The Pilgrim Fathers visited in 1620 on their way to New England. The Mayflower put in here on her way to Plymouth for repairs after being battered by a storm. The cove is very picturesque and has spectacular views of the harbour entrance. It was once used as the setting for The Onedin Line, when it was supposed to be Liverpool.

Look out for the quay, the Boatfloat, and the nearby Butterwalk, a lovely row of houses with columns built in 1635 for a Newfoundland merchant. The end house is now Dartmouth Museum. You can walk in the Royal Avenue Gardens with its colourful flowers and bandstand. Behind these gardens you can visit a building which houses an Atmospheric Engine.

The Tourist Information Bureau is also by the gardens.

4. **Continue your walk along the North Embankment. You will pass a children's play area on your left.**

5. **Cross the river by using the Upper Ferry.**

This charges a small fee, and again plies the river all day. You may have to queue in the summer.

☺ This is a chain ferry and is sometimes referred to as a floating bridge. The ferry takes you to Britannia Halt, a tiny railway station with a level crossing.

6. **At the top of the slipway turn to the right along the footpath which runs between the Great Western railway line and the river bank. The footpath ends by crossing the railway line (with great care) and you are back at the Darthaven Marina and your car.**

This is the only part of the walk which would not be possible with a double pushchair.

☺ As you walk along by the river you may see herons and oyster catchers among other birds, and you will certainly see boats of all shapes and sizes, either at their moorings, with their halyards clinking, or on the move. There is an annual regatta held every

August. Dartmouth was the scene of celebrations when Naomi James returned from her solo voyage around the world in her yacht.

In the summer you may be lucky enough to be passed by a steam train, heralded by a plume of smoke.

If you would like the opportunity to travel on one of these trains from a bygone era which run along seven miles of spectacular country between Paignton and Kingswear, telephone 01803 664313.

For a really adventurous day out it would be possible to catch the train in Paignton, then do this walk and return to Paignton by steam train!

Checklist

☐ Steam train

☐ Sailing boat

☐ Naval college

☐ Buoy

☐ Cormorant

☐ Boat house

☐ Seagull

16. Lustleigh

If you have ever wondered whether those villages on chocolate boxes really exist, now you know! Lustleigh and Pethybridge, set below the foothills of Dartmoor, are very pretty, with thatched cottages and wonderful gardens. Walkers are spoilt for choice so this walk is just a taste of the area. As for those amongst us who enjoy messing about in streams, then this is seventh heaven.

Starting point:	Park on the road by the church in Lustleigh.
Car park map reference:	785813
Distance:	About 2½ miles
Terrain:	Country lanes and rough tracks which can be muddy in places. Some steep hills.
Maps:	OS Landranger 191 and Outdoor Leisure 28, Dartmoor
By bus:	For further details phone 01752 222666.
Public Toilets:	Opposite Lustleigh Village Hall, near Village Orchard.
Telephones:	Next to Lustleigh Village Hall and in Pethybridge on the route.
Refreshments:	Tea rooms, pub and grocery stores in Lustleigh which sell snacks and ice cream.
Pushchairs:	Not possible. However, a visit to Lustleigh would be worthwhile just to potter around the village and to let the baby play on the swings and slide in Village Orchard – the prettiest play area I know!

1. **Walk around the church until you come to the post office. Walk down the lane past the Village Hall and take the path through Village Orchard. Cross the wooden footbridge and follow the track up the hill.**

☺ Village Orchard is idyllic. There are swings, a slide, a mini climbing course and a sand-pit. There are benches to sit on while admiring the apple trees and their mistletoe. Interspersed here and there are some huge, rounded granite boulders. These are typical of this area, and you will notice them throughout this walk. Running through the orchard is a lovely stream. Depending on

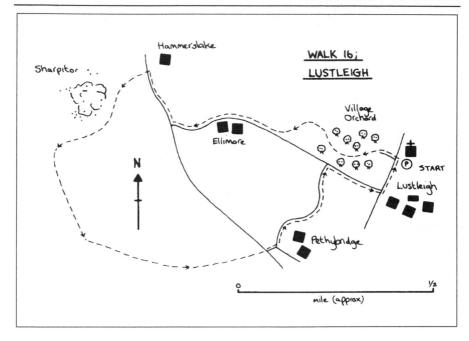

Sharpitor

Hammerslake

WALK 16;

LUSTLEIGH

Village
Orchard

Ellimore

N

START

Lustleigh

Pethybridge

0   ½

mile (approx)

the time of year there are lots of wild flowers and birds to look out for.

The largest boulder is the main focus of the May Day celebrations where the local children have a procession and dance around the Maypole. On one side of this boulder are the names of the May Queens since 1968 carved in the stone and on the top of the rock is a stone throne. The May Day celebrations take place on the first Saturday in May.

This is an ideal spot for a picnic and is a good place for children to run around and play away from traffic.

☺ Lustleigh itself is charming to explore, and has some old-fashioned shops, a gift shop, and a post office. The 13th-century church is open for visitors. The church stands at 300ft/90 metres above sea level and the surrounding hills are up to 900ft/274 metres above sea level. Lustleigh became popular in the Victorian and Edwardian eras when it was on the railway line. The railway was completed in 1866. At its peak period in the 1930s, eleven trains a day would stop in Lustleigh. There are no trains running these days.

Lustleigh

😊 The architecture in Lustleigh is varied. It is largely Victorian, but ranges from 15th-century granite and thatch to modern buildings.

2. **When this narrow track splits into three, take the right-hand path back to the stream. Cross the miniature granite clapper bridge and follow this path until you reach the road.**

😊 In places this stream almost disappears as it goes under the huge boulders.

This is a perfect place for paddling and scrambling on a fine day.

3. **Turn right onto the road and climb an extremely steep hill for about two minutes, until it, thankfully, levels out. You will pass Ellimore Farm. Keep going until you reach the T-junction.**

😊 You will be rewarded with lovely views of the surrounding hills and pretty fields, often with lambs, cattle and horses, and lush countryside full of wild flowers. As you go up the hills you gain a different perspective on Lustleigh. Again it is fun to look at the houses and imagine living in them.

As you pass the farm at Ellimore, look out for the chickens scratching about, and perhaps you may see their magnificent "Kellogg's Cornflakes" cockerels. Also have a look at the granite drinking trough.

4. **At the T-junction turn right.**

5. **Shortly you will come to a public bridleway on your left. Walk up this sunken path between hedge banks until you reach a sign post.**

☺ This track can be muddy, but it is like entering a secret dark world.

6. **At the sign take the left route for Heavens Gate for Lustleigh.**

☺ You will be climbing up through mixed deciduous woodland, an English jungle! All the way along this section of the walk you will see the characteristic boulders. Every so often you will catch glimpses of the valley way below and of the moors.

7. **The track now starts to descend. At the next sign take the left track to Manaton via Water. The route is now a steep, down-hill, rough track so take care.**

☺ If you stop and listen you can just hear the river in the distance, as well as all the birds, and often the wind in the trees. You are now in Lustleigh Cleave. The word "cleave" means "split". There is a fault running through this valley which, in conjunction with the weathering processes, has formed this dramatic valley with the granite exposed, hence all the rounded granite boulders.

8. **At the next sign head left for Lustleigh via Pethybridge. Keep left, ignoring a track to your right.**

☺ See how many trees you can recognise. This is a fantastic bluebell wood in May. The bulbs of bluebells were once used for glue and the starch from the bulbs was also used by the Elizabethans to stiffen their ruffs!

9. **Keep left, following the bridleway for Lustleigh. After a while you will come to some stables, and then onto the road.**

☺ At this point you will see some thatched roofs ahead.

10. Turn right onto this road and then left for Pethybridge.

☺ Pethybridge is picturesque, with some thatched cottages and pretty gardens. Look for another granite trough.

11. Turn right at the whitewashed, thatched cottage. Take the next right and then the next left for Lustleigh.

☺ You will see Lustleigh and the Village Orchard below, and perhaps hear the church bells coming up into the hills. This is a lovely end to the walk, coming from what seems like a secret wilderness and then gradually easing back into a more familiar world with houses and gardens in this beautiful hilly countryside. It is all the more pleasant to appreciate as you are now walking downhill.

☺ Just before you enter Lustleigh, look for the leat and sluice gate on your right.

12. Lustleigh itself is well worth exploring at leisure – you could perhaps take some well-earned refreshment, maybe at the renowned Primrose Tea Rooms.

Like most pretty Devon villages, Lustleigh is popular in the summer, but you, at least, can get away from the madding crowd by walking on.

Checklist

☐ Thatched cottages

☐ Apple tree

☐ Mistletoe

☐ Stone throne

☐ Blue bell

☐ Fox glove

☐ Granite trough

☐ Cockerel

17. Mount Edgecumbe

This is a splendid walk which starts and finishes with a ferry boat ride, making this even more of an adventure. Mount Edgecumbe will appeal to adults and children alike, with beaches and gardens, an elegant house, lakes and fountains and even a geyser! I could not resist including this walk even though Mount Edgecumbe is in Cornwall. I justify it as the start and finish are in Devon, just across the water.

Starting point:	Admirals Hard, Stonehouse, Plymouth. Follow signs firstly to the Brittany Ferries port, and then to the Cremyll Ferry for foot passengers. Park in a nearby car park. To reach Mount Edgecumbe by road take the Torpoint Car Ferry to Antony on the A374, then go to Mount Edgecumbe on the B3247.
Car park map reference:	463539
Distance:	About 2½ miles
Terrain:	Paths with reasonably good surfaces. Some hills.
Maps:	OS Sheet 201, Plymouth and Launceston
By bus:	For details phone 01752 222666
Public Toilets:	Next to The Vine Pub at Admirals Hard. Near the Edgecumbe Arms at Cremyll. By the Orangery Restaurant (with baby changing facilities) and in Mount Edgecumbe House (the toilets here are well worth a visit in their own right!)
Telephones:	Near the ferry at Admirals Hard and Cremyll
Refreshments:	Café and a pub at Admirals Hard. Snack bar and pub at Cremyll. Orangery Restaurant, open between April and October. Small tea rooms in the main house. For further details about Mount Edgecumbe phone 01752 822236. Gift shop and information centre at the entrance to the park near Cremyll. Further gift shop in the house.
Pushchairs:	Possible for the whole route, although one hill is good exercise!

1. **Catch the Cremyll ferry from Admirals Hard to Cremyll. Wait for the ferry on the slipway. Payment is for single fares when you reach Cremyll.**

The Cremyll Ferry runs approximately every half hour throughout the day, but times do vary according to the season. For details phone 01752 822105. The trip will take about 7 minutes and gives superb views of Mayflower Marina and the naval buildings of Stonehouse, and then of Mount Edgecumbe itself.

Catching the ferry at Admiral's Hard (Jamie Stewart)

☺ There may well be lots of other boats out on the water. On your left as you leave Admiral's Hard, the block of fine buildings you see are the Royal William Victualling Yard, built by the same architect who built the Plymouth Breakwater, John Rennie. They were completed in 1831. The buildings are arranged around a tidal basin through which most of the supplies would have come and gone. There was a brewery, a bakery, a flour mill and a slaughterhouse. The Victualling Yard was the caterer for the Royal Navy and the dockyards.

2. **Take the path from Cremyll into the grounds of Mount Edgecumbe Park. Walk to the Visitors Centre, and then bear left to the Orangery.**
   The Visitors Centre is a good source of information about the area, and also sells gifts and postcards. Outside there is an information board and a map.

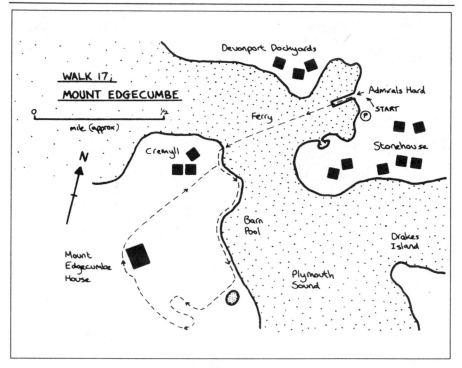

☺ As you walk towards the Orangery, look up to your right to see the house above you and the wide, tree-lined avenue. The Orangery would have once housed orange trees, as its name suggests. Now it is a restaurant. In front of the Orangery is the formal Italian Garden, with a mermaid, fountain and some statues.

3. Follow the path back to the coast, passing Thompson Seat, the Block House and the Battery.

☺ Thompson Seat is a grand covered seating area with excellent views of Plymouth Sound and the Dockyards. If you hear the wailing of an air raid siren do not be alarmed as this merely marks the shifts at Devonport Dockyard. But imagine what it must have been like during the war, particularly being so close to an area of such strategic importance. Mount Edgecumbe House was gutted by incendiary bombs in 1941, and was later restored by the Earl of Mount Edgecumbe.

The Block House was built for defence in the time of Henry the

Eighth. The Battery was built for saluting, and was remounted with the cannons in 1880. These cannons were taken from a French frigate. The views from here of Plymouth Sound and Drake's Island are excellent.

4. **Take the path to the Great Ilex Hedge and go through, either at its beginning or middle, to explore the English, French, New Zealand and American Gardens. Return to the coastal path to continue.**

☺ The Ilex, which forms these impressive hedges, is a species of evergreen oak. The gardens interlink with each other and vary in style, with many beautiful and exotic plants. Be sure not to miss the geyser which shoots up at regular intervals in the New Zealand Garden.

5. **Follow the path alongside Barn Pool to the Amphitheatre and Milton's Temple.**

☺ The beaches at Barn Pool and Cremyll are a mixture of pebbles and sand, with the odd rock pool, depending on the tide. You may see diving boats as there is some deep water just off Barn Pool which is good for this purpose.

On your route you will pass some trees planted as memorials, which I think is a lovely idea. The Amphitheatre is a fantastic piece of landscaping, with Milton's Temple and the lake combining to give a picture of perfection. On the lake you may see ducks and moorhens, and in the summer, water lilies and dragonflies.

6. **Take the uphill path beside the lake inland. At the junction take the left up the rough path which will zigzag to the right. Follow the main path to the house and gardens.**

☺ This part of the walk has a wonderful mixture of native and exotic trees, notably beeches, rhododendrons and azaleas, as well as over 600 species of camellias which were a gift from New Zealand. This is also a good place to look for wild flowers. It seems really peaceful here, but if you stop and listen you will still hear the noises from the water of this busy port.

7. **If you wish to visit the house, turn right. If not take the path to**

the left and head back down to Cremyll, following signs to the ferry.

☺ The house was originally built between 1547 and 1553 by Sir Richard Edgecumbe. It was situated in his deer park. The Earl's Garden was added in the eighteenth century and contains various old and rare trees in a magnificent setting overlooking Plymouth Sound and the Tamar Estuary.

The house and Earl's Garden are open between April and October, Wednesdays to Sundays, 11am to 5pm.

☺ Below the house is a wide avenue of trees and a lovely grass slope for running about on. Mount Edgecumbe has some of the best parkland I know.

Visit in the spring or early summer for the daffodils, magnolias, camellias, rhododendrons and azaleas.

Checklist

☐ Geyser

☐ Navel Ship

☐ Sailing boat

☐ Cemelia

☐ Drakes Island

☐ Drift wood

☐ Shell

☐ Duck

18. Upstream and Downstream from Newbridge

The River Dart meanders through this wooded valley on the edge of Dartmoor with infinite variety in these few miles. There are rapids interspersed with flat or slow-flowing pools, wonderful for paddling or even swimming in during the summer. The walk will take you through woodland and areas of open, flat common ground frequented by the Dartmoor ponies and their foals.

Starting point:	Newbridge car park. From the A38 take the Ashburton turning which is also signposted to the River Dart Country Park. Follow this road past the country park, across Holne Bridge and on until you reach the Newbridge car park on the other side of the bridge. Parking is free.
Car park map reference:	712709
Distance:	Downstream to Spitchwick – about 3 miles. Upstream from Newbridge – about 4 miles.
Terrain:	The Spitchwick walk is mostly flat on good tracks, open common land or lanes. Wellies would be useful in wet weather. Upstream from Newbridge the tracks are mostly well defined but some steep sections are liable to be muddy in wet weather.
Maps:	OS Outdoor Leisure 28, Dartmoor
Information:	During the summer a National Park Information Centre is open at Newbridge.
Public Toilets:	At the Newbridge car park
Refreshments:	Ice cream vans often present at the car park.
Pushchairs:	Not possible for the routes as described, but see information sections below for alternatives.

If you park the car in the Spitchwick car park around the corner, on the road to Leusdon – map reference 713712 – it is possible to do the Spitchwick circuit, and indeed this is very pleasant. Please note that this car park, being more isolated, is a less secure place to leave your car, so do not leave any valuables in the car.

It is possible to take pushchairs for a short walk upriver from Newbridge. Take the road which runs by the side of the car park and then the track which branches off to the left and goes across the common and through the woodland. This is a wide and slightly bumpy track but perfectly feasible.

Newbridge

Newbridge to Spitchwick

1. **From the car park, walk to the bridge and go down the steps to the river, signposted to "Picnic Area Deeper Marsh". The path goes between the river on your right and a fenced field on your left. Cross the little brook and walk down the hill onto the Deeper Marsh area of Spitchwick Common.**

☺ New Bridge was originally called Holne New Bridge, and Holne Bridge was then called Holne Old Bridge. Both bridges date from the early 15th century, but Holne Bridge was built at the site of an earlier bridge that was washed away in a flood in 1413.

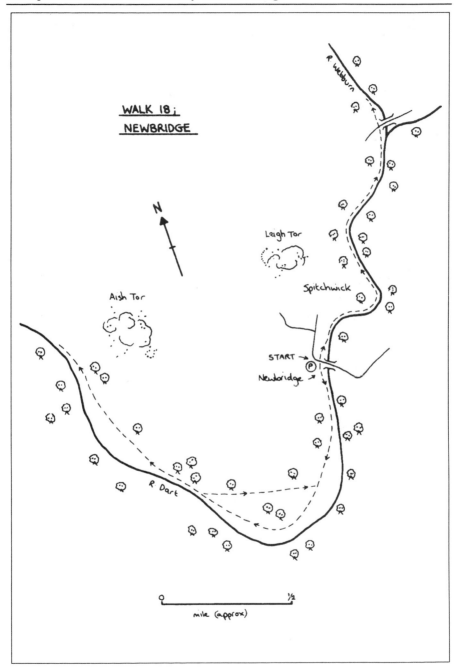

WALK 18;
NEWBRIDGE

N

R Webburn

Leigh Tor

Spitchwick

Aish Tor

START →
Newbridge →

R. Dart

0   ½
mile (approx)

During the 2nd World War a Bailey Bridge, named after the inventor, was built to stop heavy military traffic damaging New Bridge. This Bailey bridge was built from wooden planks and steel girders.

2. Walk beside the river downstream until you reach the road.

☺ This is a lovely walk at all times of year. Between October and February you may see colourful kayaks and canoes as they brave this fun section of river known as The Loop.

In the frosty weather this is a real winter wonderland with every surface coated in ice crystals, frozen ponds and icicles. In the fog there is a mystical atmosphere and all the cobwebs on the gorse bushes look as if they are draped with jewels. As for the spring, at that time everything is incredibly green, and in the autumn the golds and oranges of the trees are superb, particularly when reflected in the water. On hot summer days this is a popular picnic and barbecue spot, with children paddling and swimming, playing ball and frisbee.

3. Turn right along the road, passing the lodges. Take the right-hand fork and continue along the lane to Buckland Bridge. From here you can walk a short distance along the River Webburn if you wish. Return to Newbridge by the same route, or if you are in a hurry you can walk back along the road, but take care with the traffic.

Although this section of the walk is on country roads, it is very pleasant and not normally very busy.

☺ The junction where the River Webburn joins the River Dart is very pretty, and walking up beside the Webburn you are in beautiful woodland where you will see a wealth of wild birds, and usually lots of holly trees in the autumn with their bright berries.

Upstream from Newbridge

1. **From the car park, head to the river and then follow the track across the common beside the river. Once you have crossed a brook by stepping stones, turn right to join the main track.**

☺ You should see ponies and their foals along this stretch, as well as squirrels and rabbits. The woodland is mixed, including beech, oak, sycamore, elderflower, hawthorn and hazel. "Dart" is the Celtic word for "oak". The drystone walls are rich with moss and navelworts, and the trees have ivy entwining its way up their trunks and lichen on their branches.

2. **Follow the track, passing a pond on your right and a field used for horse jumping, until you come to a left-hand fork. This takes you back to the river and another field with horse jumping equipment.**

☺ Look for the bath in the corner of the second horse jumping field – presumably it is used as a trough rather than a horse bath!

The river here is very pretty with boulder fields and rapids, depending on the water level. In the summer this is a lovely place for a paddle or a swim, far less crowded than the better known Spitchwick, and only a leisurely 15 minutes walk from the car park. You will see a rickety bridge which you are forbidden to cross, even if you actually wanted to. By the river banks there is heather and gorse growing.

3. **Continue along the track, passing a flat, grassy area used as a picnic spot, with an empty leat on the other side. Follow the river until you rejoin the main track. Just before you reach a partial concrete bridge across this tributary there is a narrow, steep path which takes you above the river before dropping back down, and then climbing again. You will come to a cliff overlooking the river with a blue nylon rope to assist you down to a metal ladder and down to a natural platform.**

☺ This is a lovely stretch, particularly when the sun is shining through the trees and glinting on the water.

You need to take great care going down to the ladder, but if you are all reasonably sure-footed this should not be a problem and this section gives the walk an adventurous feel.

☺ The water looks as dark as ink and you get a good view from here of the rapids, which canoeists brave out of fishing season, in the winter months.

Although it is possible to walk all the way to Dartmeet, I feel that this is a good point to turn back to the car park due to the distance you will travel to get back. The path is also quite a scramble in places beyond this point.

4. **Return to Newbridge by the same route or by making more use of the main track which is shorter and will take you out onto the road which runs back to the car park.**

    The main track will take you along the other side of the dry leat which you may have noticed on the way upstream. As you follow the river, look out for dippers and wagtails, and perhaps the occasional wild duck.

Checklist

☐ Canoe or Kayak - Do you know the difference?

☐ Holly tree

☐ Crab apple tree

☐ Fish

☐ Navel wort

☐ Heather

☐ Lichen

☐ Dartmoor pony

19. Noss Mayo

This circuit takes you around the pretty fishing village of Noss Mayo,
with wonderful views first of the Yealm Estuary, and then out to sea,
the Great Mew Stone, Wembury and as far as Rame Head in
Cornwall. In the distance you should be able to make out the
Eddystone Lighthouse.

Starting point:	Car park beside the tennis courts in Noss Mayo. Noss Mayo is approached by taking the A379 from Plymouth or Kingsbridge. At Yealmpton take the B3186, signposted to Newton Ferrers and Noss Mayo. Go into Noss Mayo. At the top of the hill on the right is St Peter's Church. Go down the hill and straight over the crossroads at the bottom. In front of you on the left are the tennis courts and just before is the free car park.
Car park map reference:	547475
Distance:	About 4 miles
Terrain:	Country roads and footpaths, some liable to be muddy. Varying gradients, none too taxing, the worst hill being one which you descend.
Maps:	OS Landranger 201, Plymouth and Launceston
By bus:	For details phone 01752 222666.
Public Toilets:	At the head of Newton Creek, just before you reach the Old Ship Inn.
Refreshments:	The Old Ship Inn, The Swan Inn on the other side of the creek and there is a post office stores in Noss Mayo, on the other side of the creek and up the hill.
Pushchairs:	Would be possible with a narrow wheel-based pushchair and two adults to negotiate the occasional obstacle. Some parts would be rather bumpy, and due to the length of the walk it may be a bit of an endurance test for the adults. Noss Mayo and Newton Ferrers would be good to explore with pushchairs, even if you do not attempt this walk.

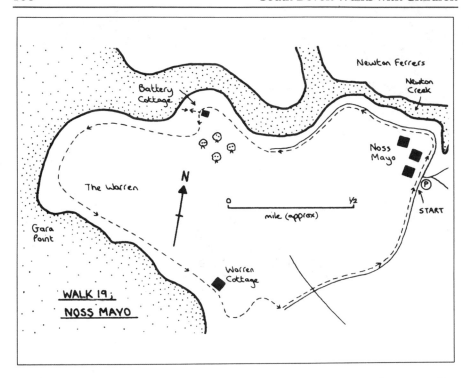

Newton Ferrers

Newton Creek

Battery Cottage

Noss Mayo

N

The Warren

0 ————————————— ½
mile (approx)

START

Gara Point

Warren Cottage

WALK 19;

NOSS MAYO

1. **Go down the hill and turn left down the steep lane to the Methodist church. Take the road beside Newton Creek, passing the Old Ship Inn on your right. Follow around the creek until you come to a sign to the coastal footpath.**

☺ As you walk past the creek you can see the church above you on the right, and ahead of you is Newton Ferrers church. It is a lovely sound if you happen to be walking when the church bells are ringing as the sound reverberates around the valley.

You can cross the creek by the walkway or "Voss" if you wish to explore Noss Mayo. There is also another of these walkways across to Newton Ferrers which is possible at low tide.

☺ Newton Ferrers is named after the Ferrers family, notorious because in 1760 the 4th Earl was the last nobleman to be hanged. He had shot his land agent dead in a fit of temper.

During this section of the walk you pass pretty cottages and boat houses, boats either moored or sailing and people fishing or merely messing about on the river. The villages grew up mainly around the fishing and crabbing industries. There may be ducks, seagulls, herons and possibly an egret if you are lucky. An egret looks like a small heron and is white.

2. Follow the coastal footpath.

You will pass a slipway which leads to a ferry which runs in the summer, weather permitting, to Newton Ferrers and Wembury.

☺ Earlier this century there were regular visits from paddle steamers. After this you pass some beautiful cottages with pretty gardens overlooking the water. One house you pass is the Toll House with the old ferry fees painted on the walls. See how much it used to cost to ferry a pony or an ass!

The tracks through woodland afford you tantalising glimpses of the water. The Yealm Estuary is actually a Ria, otherwise known as a flooded river valley. Yealm is pronounced "Yam" by the locals.

3. On your right just before you reach Battery Cottage is a steep path going down to your right to a pleasant beach. For the purpose of this walk, carry straight on in front of Battery Cottage, following the path along the coast.

☺ Battery Cottage is a beautiful place and its views must be superb. Notice all its chimney pots. The walk is now above fields with sheep, horses and cattle grazing. You get good views of the Mew Stone and Wembury from here.

When you reach the top of the hill you are on the Warren, so named as it was once used for breeding rabbits, both for eating and for their skins. You may well see wild rabbits grazing along with the sheep. I was surprised to learn that rabbits are not actually native to this country. They were confined to the Iberian Peninsula and parts of North Africa and were introduced to this country by the Norman invaders. The rabbits were for a long time actually farm animals and an important part of the rural economy. They were looked after by the warrener. Rabbits, of course, breed very efficiently and soon became plentiful in the wild. (A female rabbit may well produce about 20 young in a year and her offspring can breed when they are only four months old. Phew!) In 1954 the awful disease myxomatosis was introduced to control their numbers. Myxomatosis is a viral disease spread by fleas. As well as a dramatic decline in the rabbit population, the rabbits' predators also declined, such as foxes, stoats and buzzards. Now rabbits are common as they have developed a resistance to the disease so the food chain has also benefited. On the down side, however, rabbits are again being seen as pests because they eat crops.

The grazing rabbits are responsible for the short-cropped appearance of this strip of coastline. Look out for their burrows. (If you see their hard droppings you will know that these have already been eaten once. The first droppings are soft. The rabbits eat these while underground in their burrows, so absorbing all the goodness. The second droppings are then deposited outside the burrow.) The short turf encourages low-growing plants such as vetches, trefoils. and heather, thistles and gorse. These plants attract butterflies and other insects, which in their turn attract birds, like stonechats, linnets and finches. This makes me wonder what our country would look like if the Normans had not invaded, bringing with them their rabbits. What a chain of events, with history having a major ecological effect!

This is a beautiful section of jagged coastline, ever changing depending on the weather and tide. Beyond Wembury is HMS Cambridge, with its firing ranges, and beyond that is Rame Head in Cornwall. Far out to sea is the Eddystone Lighthouse, long since automatic. Its signal is two flashes in quick succession every ten seconds. The light is at 40 metres above sea level. If you have been to Berry Head you will have seen the squat-looking lighthouse which gains its height advantage by standing on a 60 metre high cliff, whereas the Eddystone lighthouse gains its height thanks to its building.

The Mew Stone is now owned by the Ministry of Defence, but once upon a time it was home to a family. A man was found guilty of a petty crime and was sentenced to be transported to the Mew Stone for seven years. There he stayed with his family until he had finished his sentence, when he returned to the mainland. His daughter, Black Bess, stayed. She married and had three children there, but tragedy hit when her husband died when he fell off a rock and drowned. The Mew Stone is a notorious spot for shipwrecks.

There are some welcome benches to sit on as you reach the top of the hill, ideal for admiring the views or perhaps to watch racing yachts. As you round the headland to Gara Point there are

Coastal footpath along "The Warren" near Noss Mayo

beautiful grassy slopes heading down to the sea, so plenty of choices for the perfect picnic spot.

4. **Go through the gate next to Warren Cottage. Follow the road to the left instead of the coastal footpath. Head inland through the gate and walk up this lane until you reach a car park and the road.**

☺ Notice the unusual gateposts outside the house.

5. **At the road turn left.**

6. **Almost immediately turn right onto a footpath signposted to Noss Mayo. This takes you downhill into Noss Mayo and to the car park, just beyond the tennis courts on your right.**

    This part of the walk takes you past fields where you may see cattle or sheep, perhaps chickens and geese, or crops.

Checklist

☐ Rabbit

☐ Sailing boat

☐ Rowing boat

☐ Rabbit droppings

☐ Eddystone lighthouse

☐ Heron

☐ Gorse

☐ Mewstone

20. Parke, Bovey Tracey

Here you will have a peaceful stroll along the old railway track, and
then return beside the River Bovey. It changes as the seasons alter
the mood of the woodlands. This is a good walk for studying nature,
so look, listen and smell. The old railway track is good for cycles — flat,
with a reasonable, if slightly bumpy, surface and no cars!

Starting point:	Park your car near Hole Bridge on the side of the Bovey Tracey to Moretonhampstead Road (A382).
Car park map reference:	811785
Distance:	About 2 miles
Terrain:	Mostly level. Well-defined paths and the old railway track. The riverside tracks can be muddy in wet weather.
Maps:	Landranger 191, Okehampton and North Dartmoor
Public Toilets:	None. The nearest are in Bovey Tracey.
Refreshments:	None. Good spots by the river for picnics.
Pushchairs:	Possible for most of route as described as long as you return to the old railway track opposite the bridge, near the maze.

1. **If you are facing in the direction of Moretonhampstead, you head through the kissing gate on your left onto the footpath and turn to your right. Once you are on the path you are on the old railway line. Follow this until its end.**

☺ The track takes you through the lovely woodland. The trees are
mostly deciduous, including beech, chestnut, birch, elder, ash.
sycamore, lime, hazel and larch. In the hedge near where you
left the car is guelder rose which is very attractive with its bright
berries in late summer and autumn.

The railway line went to Moretonhampstead but was closed in
1959. Since that time, nature has slowly reclaimed its territory.
Depending on the time of year, there are plenty of wild flowers to
look out for, including primroses, foxgloves, wood anemones,
Himalayan balsam, hemp-agrimony, fleabane, tansy, knapweed
and the purple orchids. Hemp-agrimony is tall with red stems and

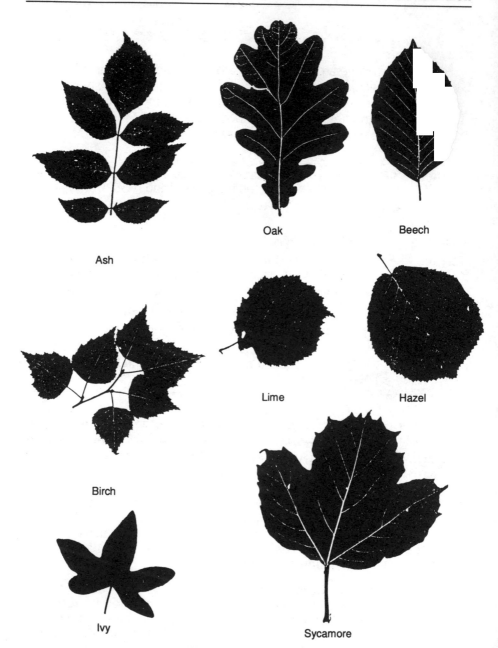

Ash

Oak

Beech

Birch

Lime

Hazel

Ivy

Sycamore

Outlines of leaves to be found on this walk

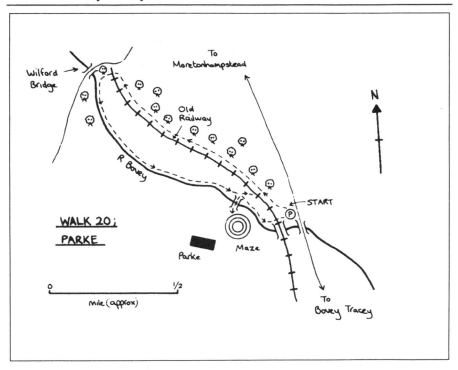

WALK 20;
PARKE

pink florets and is found beside the river. It has medicinal properties and has been used as a cure for jaundice, and also has good wound-healing properties. It had to be used with caution, however. Fleabane was once used to get rid of fleas by burning it. Tansy, with its bright yellow flower, is common throughout Britain on waste ground and roadsides, and as such is ignored as a weed. However, it was once valued as a flavouring for omelettes and cakes, Tansy cake being popular at Easter. The leaves were used for these culinary purposes, but these days we tend to prefer the spices such as cinnamon and nutmeg, which were once hard to come by and expensive as they were imported. It was also used as a deterrent to mice and flies. It has also been used as a mouth wash, an eye lotion and a cosmetic. Knapweed resembles a thistle, with a pink-purple flower. It has been used in the treatment of bruises and scabs, hence its Latin name centaurea scabiosa.

In the summer there are lots of butterflies, moths, dragon flies and damselflies. Also, in the air you might see the buzzards, or hear their mewing cry. There are many other small birds in these woods such as wrens, robins, wagtails and blackbirds.

This is ideal country for the grey squirrels. You may well see them eating hazel nuts or the signs that they have been munching — many of the nuts on the ground are partly eaten!

As you start along the railway track there is a beautiful house through the trees to your right with an idyllic garden with a stream running through it. A little further along to your left, in the distance through the trees, you can make out Parke House, now the headquarters of the Dartmoor National Park. It was built in the 1820s and replaced an earlier building that had been built in the 14th century. Parke was owned by the Hole family for over 200 years, until Major Hole died in 1974 leaving the house and land to the National Trust. There are various legends surrounding this place including a white rabbit which appears in June and is said to be the spirit of a dead bride.

Towards the end of this stretch you will pass beneath a limestone bridge with the calcite formations associated with caves — stalactites. Imagine the scene back at the beginning of this century when a cart carrying a lion belonging to a circus got stuck on the Wilford Bridge.

2. **Just before you reach the road, turn left down a slope to the river. Follow the path beside the river downstream until you come to Parke Bridge. This is a charming trail over and around tree trunks with wooden bridges over streams.**

There are several little sandy beaches and parts of the river which are just right for paddling. There are also a few deeper pools where you could take a swim.

☺ There are several weirs — the third is the largest and has some benches beside it so is a good spot to stop for rest or play and perhaps take some photographs.

In medieval times the river was panned for tin. Nowadays you may spot salmon and sea trout. You will pass several meadows, lovely for their wild flowers, including orchids. The flowers attract various species of butterflies.

The weir on the River Bovey (Angie Abbott)

3.   At the bridge take a short detour by crossing it and taking the gate on your left marked "Enclosure".

☺ Here you will find a maze made out of wooden stakes which is good fun.

If you have a pushchair, return to the old railway up a short slope on your left, shortly before the bridge. Once back on the railway line retrace your steps back to the car. A lightweight, narrow pushchair would be most suitable for this walk — to negotiate tree roots and narrow bridges.

4.   Having returned to the path beside the river, cross the wooden stile and bridge across a tributary. Climb up the steps cut into the rock face and follow the track back down to the river. Follow the river until you reach the bridge. Climb over the stile, up the steps or short, steep slope to the railway line and out through the gate to your car, remembering this is a busy road.

Checklist

☐ Butterfly or moth

☐ Fish

☐ Orchid

☐ Primrose

☐ Blackberry

☐ Wood anemone

☐ Stalactite

☐ Horse

21. Sharpitor to Starehole Bay near Salcombe

This reminds me of my favourite sort of walk, high up in the mountains, even though this is a coastal walk. You should get a real sense of achievement without it actually being too demanding. This dramatic walk shows you some of the finest coastal scenery around and includes a visit to an idyllic beach should the tide and weather permit.

Starting point:	Sharpitor near Salcombe. Sharpitor is signposted from Kingsbridge and Salcombe, and is 1½ miles south-west of Salcombe. In the summer the National Trust makes a charge for parking. You could also park in the South Sands car park, also for a charge. Park either in the lanes approaching the Overbecks Museum and Garden, or in its car park near the gates to the gardens.
Car park map reference:	727375
Distance:	About 2 miles
Terrain:	Undulating, rough, narrow, well-defined tracks. Some parts may be muddy in wet weather.
Maps:	OS Outdoor Leisure 20, South Devon
By bus:	To Salcombe. For further details phone 01752 222666.
Public Toilets:	South Sands
Refreshments:	Tea rooms at Overbecks Museum, Sharpitor, if you are visiting the house. Pub at South Sands. I would recommend that you bring your own refreshments.
Pushchairs:	Not possible

1. **Walk up the hill to the entrance to the Overbecks Museum. Continue climbing, passing the garden walls. Follow signs to Sharp Tor or Bolt Head.**

   Overbecks Museum and Gardens are run by the National Trust. The gardens are beautiful with many rare shrubs, plants and trees, and superb views over the Salcombe Estuary. The house is

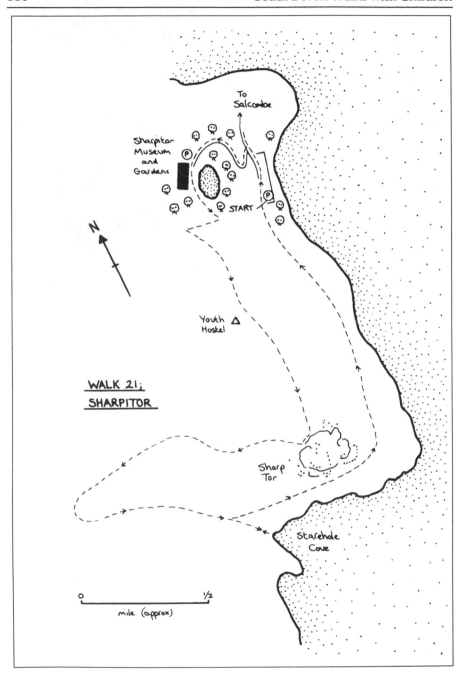

To Salcombe

Sharpitor Museum and Gardens

START

Youth Hostel △

WALK 21;
SHARPITOR

Sharp Tor

Starehole Cove

N

0   ½
mile (approx)

Lower path to Sharpitor

Edwardian and contains collections of old photographs of the area, local shipbuilding tools and model boats as well as shells, toys and others collections. There is also an exhibition of the National History of Sharpitor. For further details phone 01548 842893 or 843238.

☺ The track heads off to the left up some steps. You will then find yourselves between hedgerows on the left and a field to your right. There is a trig point on your right which is at 428 metres above sea level. Every so often you will gain tantalising glimpses of the estuary below. Across the fields you can make out the Coast Guard Station near Higher Soar.

2.   When you reach some rocky outcrops you are at Sharp Tor.

☺ Now you will find that all the uphill climbing was worthwhile as the views are superb and the rugged rock formations are very beautiful and dramatic. You will see that this rocky outcrop is aptly named. There is an orientation pillar which points you in the direction of Plymouth, Eddystone Lighthouse, Cherbourg and Exeter, among other places. It also indicates their distance from here.

From this point you have a bird's eye view of Salcombe, the estuary and its Bar and of Prawle Point. The Bar can be a hazard to shipping, particularly at low tide. It is probably for this reason that Salcombe is still a small harbour.

3. **Rejoin the path as it makes its way around Starehole Cove. Take the path down to the cove.**

☺ This is a fantastic stretch of path with wonderful coastal views of the cove and Bolt Head. At times you will not be able to see the sea and you could easily be fooled into thinking that you were walking amongst Dartmoor's tors. As you descend the track to the cove there are very dramatic views of the rock pinnacles above you. Much of this stretch is either relatively flat or downhill.

If you want to extend your walk to Bolt Head, follow the signs which take you up onto the headland, with its extensive views.

4. **Cross over the stile and go down the steep path to the cove.**

☺ This is an option which is well worth doing at low tide.

Just before you get down to the beach there is a stream which drips from above so this section of track is liable to be muddy. There are some metal railings and a bridge to negotiate near an attractive waterfall, and then climb with care over the rocks which can be a bit slippery.

☺ The beach has soft, golden sand, rock pools and sea caves and is one of the loveliest little beaches I can think of, and it is quite likely you will have it to yourselves. The waterfall runs on to the beach so if you enjoy damming rivers this is the place for you. Above you tower the pinnacles of rock of Sharp Tor, giving you an indication of how far you have descended. In the summer you may see water-skiing, sailing or canoeing taking place in this ideal cove.

Spare a thought, however, for the tall ship which was beached here having been wrecked on nearby rocks. She was the *Herzogin Cecille*, the world's largest windjammer and eight times winner of the grain race from Australia. She was wrecked on the 24th April 1936, carrying a cargo of corn which then started to rot and could be smelt for miles off. Thousands of people travelled to see the wreck, which was there for seven weeks. Local farmers are said to have made quite a profit by charging these visitors. Over the years there have been many wrecks off this stretch of coastline. The iron content in the cliffs has been suggested as one reason as this may have interfered with the ships' compasses. Under the sand at Starehole Cove is a submerged fossilised forest.

5. **Return to the path and follow the signs back to Sharpitor, following the coastal footpath to return to your car.**

☺ This breathtaking stretch of coastal footpath is known as the Courtenay Walk after the man who built it in the last century, the Earl of Devon, Viscount Courtenay. It is also now known as the Lower Path, as opposed to the higher path that you took on the way out. The path climbs up along the cliff, passing through the pinnacles at the top. This part is, thankfully, protected by railings. This sort of path strongly reminds me of some of the intrepid paths in the Alps, cut into the sides of mountain faces, and yet here you are overlooking the sea.

Contorted grey and green slates form this headland and these were, indeed, once part of a mountain range. There is a multitude of wild flowers to spot on this walk. In the summer you will be accompanied by the beautiful smell of wild honeysuckle. The sweet-smelling pink flowers are thrift, and are well adapted to the infertile terrain as they have very long roots which reach down to levels where there is a constant water supply. The little blue pom-pom flowers you may notice in the summer are called sheeps-bit, its name referring to the way it is cropped, or "bit", by the sheep in the rough pastures where it tends to grow. You may also see mountain cranesbill which is a sort of geranium which is usually seen in the European mountains, but which has taken to growing wild in Britain at lower levels.

As you round the corner at the top you will be afforded excellent views of Salcombe, which is very much a centre for yachting. Its name is derived from "Salt Valley" referring to the times when salt was evaporated from sea water in large pans on the beach.

Checklist

- ☐ Banana palm
- ☐ Thrift
- ☐ Sailing boat
- ☐ Shell
- ☐ Waterfall
- ☐ Sheep
- ☐ Seagull
- ☐ Trig point

22. Start Point

This is certainly as good a point as any to start from! Puns aside, Start
Point is a very striking headland with its distinctive lighthouse and
jagged rocks. During the walk you will have extensive views of Slapton
Ley and beyond in one direction, and of Prawle Point in the other.
Included in this walk is the lovely sandy beach of Great Mattiscombe
Sands so take along picnics, buckets and spades, and your swimming
things in the summer.

Starting point:	Park in the car park at the end of the lane. As this is privately owned, a charge is levied in the summer. From Kingsbridge or Dartmouth take the A379 to Stokenham and follow signs to Start Point.
Car park map reference:	821376
Distance:	About 2½ miles
Terrain:	Mostly narrow coastal footpath, with a little optional scrambling and a tarmac track. Hilly.
Maps:	OS Landranger 202, Torbay and South Dartmoor area
Public Toilets:	None
Refreshments:	None
Pushchairs:	Not possible for the route described. However, the first stretch of the walk (to the lighthouse) is possible as this is a tarmac track with a manageable gradient. This would be a total distance of just under 1 mile.

1. **From the top of the car park, go through the gate or across the
    stone stile signposted to Start Point Lighthouse. Walk down the
    tarmac track to the lighthouse.**

    ☺ From the car park you can see the BBC transmitting station with
    all its masts.

    Beside the gate is an information picture which tells you of the
    lost villages of Start Bay.

    ☺ The most famous of these lost villages was Hallsands, where
    eight houses were destroyed and ten were severely damaged

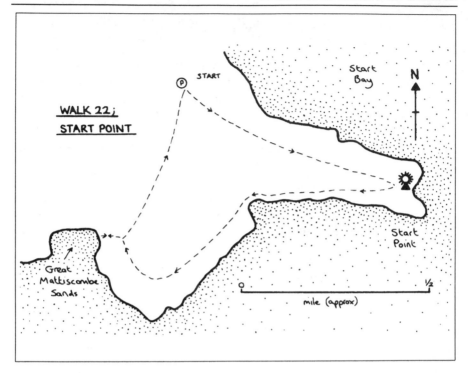

during a storm. This is said to have been caused by changed
beach levels due to dredging operations for the building of
Plymouth Breakwater. From this point you get good views of
Hallsands, Beesands, Torcross, Slapton Ley.

I always think that the name Slapton Sands is a misnomer as the
"sands" are actually rather large pebbles. The ley was formed
when the spit extended and dammed off the little river, thereby
forming a freshwater lagoon, which is now treasured for its
wildlife. Spit and bar formation is by the action of the incoming
waves from the direction of the prevailing wind.

As you walk down to the lighthouse you can enjoy the views with
the sea and Start Bay to your left and the rock pinnacles to your
right. There is often plenty of nautical activity off Start Point as
this is a popular place for races. At times of mid tide you may be
able to see the powerful tidal race and overfall off the headland,
which in canoeing terms can be like grade 2-3 white water,
therefore rough!

You can't go into the lighthouse but it is worth having a look. Be
warned, however, that the fog horn is very loud if you go down
on a foggy day. There has been a lighthouse here since 1837. It

is now automatic and is recognised by sailors as giving a light flash 3 times every 10 seconds. It is as bright as 800,000 candles. Look out for sea birds such as gulls and cormorants.

2. **Head back up the track for about 50 metres and then head up the rough track onto the rocky ridge. Follow this track along the ridge away from the lighthouse until it joins the main coastal footpath. (Alternatively if any members of your party are not particularly sure-footed or are nervous of heights, then you can continue about a quarter of a mile up the tarmac track until you see the signpost for the coastal footpath.)**

☺ The ridge walk is a superb scramble, very exciting without being too difficult, **as long as you are careful and it is not too windy.** You get a feeling of being a mountaineer up here. Look out for the thrift, white sea campions and thistles.

3. **Follow the track around the headland until you reach the sandy beach of Great Mattiscombe Sands.**

☺ This is a lovely track winding along the headland. Do look back every so often for the panorama of the rocky ridge with the

The ridge above Start Point light-house

lighthouse at the end. Below you will see an old wave cut platform, cut out by the sea when the sea level was higher, but now grass-covered ledges cropped by sheep. This is The Warren.

Start Point has its place in history as it was near here that a local girl, Ella Trout, rescued a man from the water after his boat had been torpedoed in the First World War.

Once you round Peartree Point, you will get good views of the beach and along the coast to Prawle Point which is the most southerly point of Devon. The beach is of wonderful, soft, golden sands, At the far end of the beach are two pointed rock formations, and in the middle of the beach, noticeable at low tide, is a beautiful sea-sculptured round boulder. If this were a major tourist destination, you could imagine pictures of this beach in the glossy brochures, but thankfully it is not.

Near the path is a freshwater stream which is handy for washing off sandy children before heading back to the car.

4. **The path goes directly inland up the valley, with the stone wall on your left. At the end of the track turn left, go through the gate and you are back in the car park.**

    This is the price you pay for a decent beach which is hardly ever overcrowded. It is a steady climb, not too steep, but will take about 15 minutes. It might be worth having a treat or two up your sleeve to jolly the children along on this last stretch.

Checklist

- [ ] Lighthouse
- [ ] Lagoon
- [ ] Shell
- [ ] Seaweed
- [ ] Sheep
- [ ] Seagull
- [ ] Bird of prey
- [ ] Rabbit

23. Stover Country Park

This is an easy, level walk around a pretty pond originally owned and created by James Templer in the 1700s. You will be walking in attractive woodland, with a wide variety of wildlife. There are benches to sit on and picnic tables. Do take some fresh bread with you to feed the ducks. (Mouldy bread is bad for them.)

Starting point:	Park in the pay and display car park at Stover Country Park. This is near the A38. From the Drumbridges Roundabout, take the Newton Abbot direction on the A382, taking the first left turn into the Stover Country Park.
Car park map reference:	832753
Distance:	4 miles in total but with options for shorter routes.
Terrain:	Level, well-surfaced paths around the lake, and narrow tracks in the woods, liable to be muddy in the wet weather. Bridges over waterways.
Maps:	The Information Centre at the car park supplies good maps showing the route described.
By bus:	For further details phone 01803 484950.
Public Toilets:	Near the car park, including a toilet for the disabled.
Refreshments:	Ice cream or snack vans sometimes at the car park.
Pushchairs:	Easy for the yellow route. The green route is possible if you have a narrow pushchair and don't mind manoeuvres around the odd obstacle.

1. From the car park take the track down to the lake.

☺ Stover Country Park was purchased in 1979. There are 46 hectares/114 acres and it was declared a site of Special Scientific Interest in 1984.

There are various informative notices about the area and its wildlife. By the car park is an excellent information centre. For more details phone 01626 835236/52541.

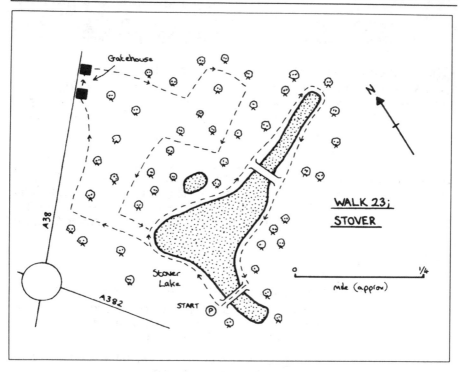

2. **Walk around the lake in a clockwise direction. Follow the yellow posts for the route which just goes around the lake and to the cascades.**

The yellow route is very pretty as you are next to the lake or waterways all the time. On the water you should see ducks, gulls, coots, moorhens, swans, and geese. If you are lucky you could also see kingfishers and woodpeckers as well.

It is likely that you will see grey squirrels and if you are really lucky, there are some deer about. There is a chance you could see lizards or snakes, and in the summer the habitat is ideal for dragonflies and butterflies. As well as the native trees there are also some exotic species, some of which were planted by James Templer. Around the lake are some areas of thick rhododendron undergrowth which lend themselves to imaginative play.

Stover Lake

3. If you are doing the longer route which takes in the woodland and the gatepost to Stover House, then you will need to follow the green posts. You will finish the green route where you started it and then you can continue the rest of the walk on the yellow route.

☺ The green route takes you through some lovely mixed woodland where you get a good idea of all the work which goes into woodland management. There are lots of nesting boxes on the trees and it is obviously an area rich in wildlife, which is reassuring considering the close proximity to the busy A38 which you can always hear but you can also ignore. Luckily, the birds seem to ignore it too. Particularly after rain, the woodland smells beautiful and fresh, of pine and peat.

This route goes as far as the gate house to Stover House. It was built in about 1780 and is fascinating with its false doors and windows and what looks like a real fire place. James Templer, the original owner, started life as an orphan in Exeter. When he was still quite young he ran away to sea. In the years to follow he made his fortune in India where he built the Madras Dock. He returned to England and in 1765 bought the estate at Stover and built Stover House, which is now a girl's school.

I enjoy this walk at all times of year. Due to its sheltered position it is a good choice in the winter. There are always ducks to feed and the scenery is lovely but changes depending on the time of year. To make a day of it you may like to combine your walk with a visit to the Trago Mills shopping complex which is just across the road. Here there are entertainments for children as well as a wide variety of shops. There are snack facilities and landscaped grounds with exotic fowl and other animals. Telephone Bickington 821111.

Checklist

☐ Squirrel

☐ Duck

☐ Swan

☐ Canadian gose

☐ Dragonfly or damselfly

☐ Woodpecker

☐ Fox

☐ Butterfly

24. Teignmouth Sea Front

This is a glorious promenade for all ages and abilities at any time of year and in all but the roughest weather conditions. You can walk as far as you wish before returning, with ample opportunity to enjoy this red sandy beach.

Starting point:	Pay and display car park on the Teignmouth to Dawlish road (A379). From Teignmouth, pass the railway station on your left and take the Dawlish road. The car park is on your right, part way up the hill.
Car park map reference:	944733
Distance:	About 2½ miles
Terrain:	Flat along the sea wall. After heavy seas there may be sand and stones on the wall. There is a big drop off the sea wall into the sea or down onto the beach depending on the state of the tide, so young children must be kept firmly under control.
Maps:	OS Landranger 192, Exeter, Sidmouth and surrounding area
By bus:	For further details phone 01803 613226, 01392 427711 or 01752 222666.
By train:	For details phone 01345 484950.
Public Toilets:	In the car park. At the start of the sea wall under the Corinthian Yacht Club.
Refreshments:	Snack bars and ice creams available on the promenade. Teignmouth town centre is within easy walking distance, too.
Pushchairs:	Possible for the whole route. Double pushchairs possible. To get down to the beach you will need to negotiate steps unless you head towards the pier for about one hundred metres from the starting point – here you will find a ramp.

1. **At the bottom of the car park, take the path to the right over the railway to the swimming Lido. Go to the sea front and turn left.**

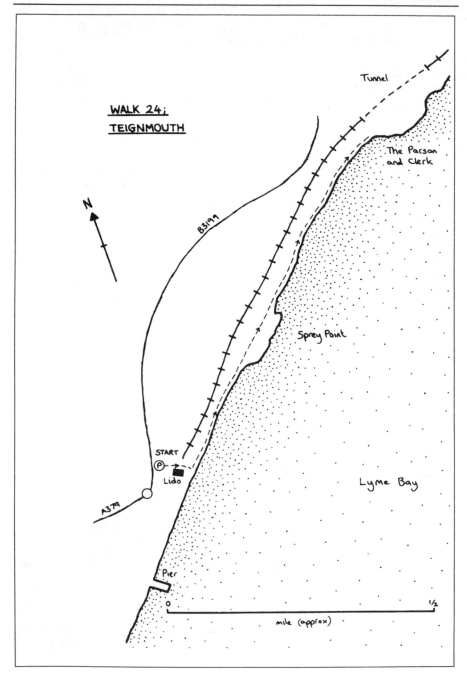

WALK 24;
TEIGNMOUTH

N

B3199

Tunnel

The Parson
and Clerk

Sprey Point

START
Lido

A379

Lyme Bay

Pier

0   ½
mile (approx)

If you would like to combine your walk with a swim, the telephone number of the lido is 01626 779063.

2. **Walk along the sea wall with the railway line on your left until the path ends at the tunnel.**

☺ The sea wall protects the railway line which was originally built in the 1840s with the trains running on Isambard Brunel's Atmospheric system. This failed because of salt water spoiling the leather valves and by 1848 conventional locomotives were used instead. Nowadays you are likely to see trains passing at regular intervals.

Teignmouth has a chequered history. Starting off as a settlement for salt makers in 600AD, it was invaded a number of times by the French and also the Danes. It was heavily bombed in the Second World War. There is even an Armada shipwreck under the sea bed only just off shore. There is a sign informing you of its presence. In the 1700s Teignmouth became popular as a health resort, and when the railway arrived it became a holiday resort.

Sprey Point is the site of a cliff fall in 1839. It was levelled out for the railway. Between the wars there was a tea house here with outside table tennis, and refreshments were wheeled along the sea wall on a cart!

Teignmouth sea wall

3.   Return by the same route.

☺ This walk along part of the coastal footpath is very dramatic with beautiful red cliffs and a red sandy beach, yet flat all the way!

It is possible to get on to the beach at various points, tide permitting.

☺ This is a great walk for train-spotting, too. Every time I have done this walk it has been different, whether with a calm, blue sea with views for miles, or rough, wet and windy with fantastic waves breaking over the path. In the rough weather there are often large ships anchored off shore to gain shelter. Sometimes we have been on our own, and at others there have been lots of people out promenading, children trying out their bikes, flying kites or roller-skating, and dogs of all breeds imaginable either walking sedately or frolicking on the beach, the more hardy taking a swim and the less brave having a paddle. Imagine the scene in the last century in the days of the bathing machines! If you look up you may see buzzards circling in the thermal currents above the cliffs.

There is ample opportunity for extending your walk by heading for the Grand Pier, where there are sea side entertainments. For further details telephone 01626 774367. Beyond the pier there is more flat promenade and beach.

Checklist

☐ Train

☐ Polished glass pebble

☐ Shell

☐ Dog

☐ Bicycle

☐ Lifebuoy

☐ Tunnel

☐ Pier

25. Bonehill, Widecombe

This is an incredibly dramatic walk giving stunning views of the surrounding moors and of Widecombe-in-the-Moor, well-known for its fair and the song. The walk starts with a fairly steep climb, which is well worth the effort, and then levels off before going back downhill to join a level track. This is not suitable for pushchairs, so as a postscript I have given a walk around the village which would be enjoyable for the whole family as well as being easy with a pushchair.

Starting point:	From Widecombe take the Bovey Tracey road. At the bottom of the hill you will cross a bridge over the East Webburn. Take the left turn for Bonehill. Drive up through this attractive hamlet and keep going until you come out onto moorland with Bonehill on your right. Park on your right below Bonehill.
Car park map reference:	731776
Distance:	About 2½ miles
Terrain:	Open moorland and a rough track. This walk involves a fairly steep climb and descent over rough terrain so sturdy shoes or boots are recommended.
Maps:	OS Outdoor Leisure 28, Dartmoor
By bus:	To Widecombe. For further details phone 01803 613226 or 01752 222666.
Public Toilets:	In Widecombe, in the main car park.
Refreshments:	In Widecombe, where there is a choice of cafés and shops, also one pub in the village itself, and another down the road by the church towards Venton.
Pushchairs:	Not possible for the Bonehill walk, but a pushchair route to explore Widecombe is given.

1. Climb up to Bonehill Rocks.

☺ The rocks of Bonehill are wonderful examples of weathered granite. If you fancy trying your hand at bouldering, that's climbing on boulders where the fall would not be great, this is an excellent spot. Otherwise, it is a super place to clamber about and admire the views of Widecombe and the surrounding hills.

Widecombe's most famous landmark is the 14th-century St Pancras Church, otherwise known as the Cathedral of the Moor. Its building was financed by the tin miners.

2.   **Follow the ridge north, crossing back over the road, and climb steeply up to Bel Tor.**

☺ Like Bonehill, Bel Tor is another great place to explore and clamber over, with its beautifully jointed granite. You will now have extensive views of the moors, including Hay Tor and Hound Tor to the east. To the west, the large rolling expanse of hill is Hameldown Down which is the home of one of the best preserved Bronze Age villages on the moors, Grimspound.

3.   **Follow on up the ridge to Chinkwell Tor.**

☺ Chinkwell Tor, you may be relieved at this point to hear, is the highest of the tors you will climb on this walk at 460 metres above sea level. To make you feel pleased with yourself, think how far you have climbed. Bonehill Rocks are at 375 metres and Widecombe itself sits at about 265 metres .

Bonehill rocks

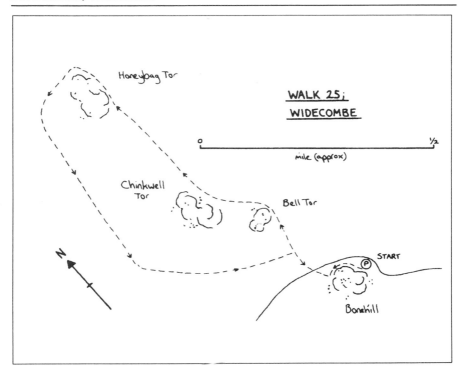

4. **Follow the ridge along to Honeybag Tor, or Honeybags as it is often called.**

☺ When I lived in Widecombe this walk was my favourite, partly because of the superb views and beautiful rock formations, and partly because of the amusing names that trigger off the imagination.

5. **Follow a green way through the bracken under the south aspect of the Tor, down the hill to the stony track. The green way may be difficult to find, in which case just head down the hill towards the track to the west taking the easiest route you can find.**

Care must be exercised here not to twist ankles on hidden rocks. Also, be aware that this is adder country because of the bracken and boulders. Do not let this put you off because these snakes are probably more frightened of us than we are of them, and noisy

foot steps will probably scare them off. If you are interested, I
have added a few facts about them. If not, skip quickly on to 6.

☺ Adders, also known as vipers, are Britain's commonest snake,
and the only ones which are poisonous. The bite is, however,
rarely fatal but would need urgent hospital treatment. Every so
often they shed their skins, so cast skins may indicate their
presence. They eat mice, voles, lizards, frogs and toads, but they
don't need a feast every day as a good meal can keep them going
for about a week. They kill their prey with poison fangs, which
they sensibly move out of the way before swallowing. They have
loosely hinged, wide-opening jaws. Female adults usually
become pregnant once every two years after a courtship in April,
and the fully formed young, perhaps 15 to 20 of them at a time,
are born in August or September. The mother doesn't look after
the young, although they may hide under her. It will take 2 to 3
years before the adders reach maturity and they can live for 9 to
10 years. Females are longer than the males, perhaps as long
as 75 centimetres (30 inches). The females are fatter and
browner than the males but with less clear markings. In the winter
the adders will go into hibernation in a cool dry place, often
sharing with some others. Adders are recognised by their
distinctive dark zigzag markings along their backs whereas grass
snakes have a plain back with some spots, particularly on their
flanks. Grass snakes are more common than adders and totally
harmless to humans. Has that given you shudders down the
spine? It has me!

6.   **Once you reach the track turn to the left and head back to your
     car.**

☺ This track is actually an ancient road from Natsworthy to
Ashburton called Thornhill Lane.

This is a pleasant end to the walk with good views below where
you have just walked. To your right, take this opportunity to
admire the drystone wall which is characteristic of Dartmoor.
Dry stone walls are of granite, and as their name suggests, that
is all they are made of — there is no cement to stick the rocks
together.

Pushchair route

Although this route is for pushchairs, it is actually well worth doing as a way of exploring Widecombe-in-the-Moor.

Starting point:	Main car park in Widecombe. Parking is free.
Car park map reference:	718769
Distance:	About 2 miles
Terrain:	Tarmac lanes
Maps:	As for the main walk
Public Toilets:	By the car park
Telephone:	By the car park
Refreshments:	Pub, cafés and a post office which doubles as a general stores.

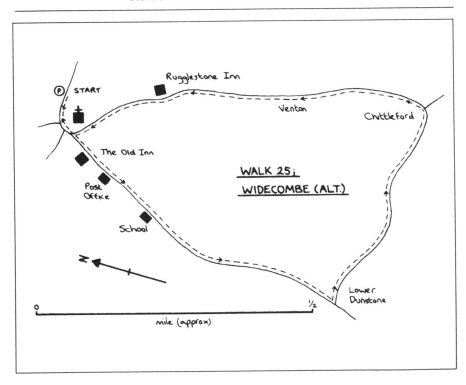

1. **Explore the village with its gift shops and resident Dartmoor ponies.**

☺ Widecombe lies in the East Webburn valley.

The church is open for visitors and supplies leaflets about its history.

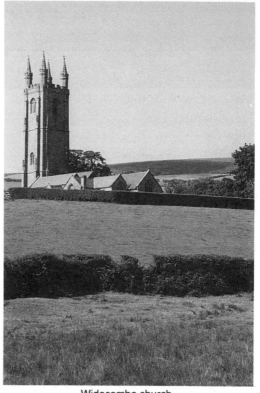

Widecombe church

☺ When you are in the church, do look up to see the bosses in the ceiling. It is said that the devil once paid a visit to this church. It is also where I was married! The graveyard is home to the grave of Olive Katherine Parr who was a local authoress who wrote under the name of Beatrice Chase. She was also known as the Lady of the Moor. She claimed that she was a descendant of Catherine Parr, Henry the Eighth's sixth wife.

Next to the church is the Church House, built in 1537 to provide rest and refreshment for weary travellers who had come a long way for the church services. It is now owned by the National Trust, which has a small shop here.

The Old Inn sells food and accepts children.

☺ It also boasts a ghost called Harry who is usually seen mid-afternoon!

2. **Go down the hill, past the post office and then the school. Keep going along this road until you reach the first turning left which you take to Lower Dunstone.**

   This part of the walk can be a bit busy, so take care and walk on the right so as to face the oncoming traffic.

   ☺ The field on your left opposite the school is the home to the main events of the famous Widecombe Fair, which is held on the second Tuesday of September. Do any of you know the song about Old Uncle Tom Cobley and All?

3. **Turn left at Lower Dunstone and keep going until you reach Chittleford Cross.**

   ☺ This is a much quieter road so you can enjoy extensive views of the surrounding hills above, and the peaceful sights of cattle grazing in the fields. The hedgerows are rich with wild flowers, notably violets, primroses and snowdrops in the spring.

4. **At Chittleford Cross turn left. Pass the hamlet of Venton and later the Rugglestone Pub. Follow the road up the hill to the church and back to the car park.**

   ☺ The farmhouses at Chittleford and Venton are examples of longhouses, where the granite building shares a central entrance and passage, with the family living on one side and the animals in the other, all sharing the same entrance. Shilstone Rocks Stud at Chittleford breeds pure Dartmoor ponies, as well as supplying pony trekking and pony and trap lessons. Venton was once the home of Beatrice Chase and you can see her disused chapel as you pass. My husband and I enjoyed living in Venton for three years so can recommend its hospitality.

   The Rugglestone Pub is full of its own special character. The drinks are served in the front room of the house which is very popular with the locals and there is a good chance you may meet Uncle Tom Cobley here!

   As Widecombe is in the Dartmoor National Park it is protected so it is unlikely to suffer great change and be ruined by widespread new housing. If you visit Widecombe in the summer you will be among many tourists, or "grockles" as they are called locally. However, you can still get away from the madding crowd on this walk.

Checklist

☐ Granite tor

☐ Long house

☐ Sheep

☐ Pony

☐ Heather

☐ Granite Cross

☐ Rowan tree

☐ Old Uncle Tom Cobbley and All

Bibliography

Village Walks in Britain, AA/Ordnance Survey

Walking the Stories and Legends of Dartmoor, Michael Bennie *(Peninsula)*

Cockington, Jo Connell *(Obelisk)*

South Devon and Dartmoor, Raymond B. Cottell

The Dart Valley (Dartmoor National Park)

Hour's Stroll on Dartmoor, John Hayward *(Curlew)*

Dartmoor National Park, HMSO

South Devon Coast Path, Brian Le Messurier *(Countryside Commission)*

Exploring England's Heritage: Devon and Cornwall, Andrew Saunders

The Devon Village Book, (Countryside Books)

Walks for Motorists on Dartmoor, Brian Le Messurier (Warne Gerrard)

Walks for Motorists S. Devon, Alan Cole (Warne Gerrard)

Secret Waters, John Watney (Bloomsbury)

Burrator, Peter Walsh and Brian Byng

Walks 2, Dartmoor National Park (Devon Books)

South Devon and Dartmoor, Ordnance Survey (Jarrold)

Dartmoor Walks, Ordnance Survey (Jarrold)

Widecombe, Michael Williams (Bossiney)

Dartmoor Seasons, Dartmoor National Park (Devon Books)

Also of interest:

BEST PUB WALKS IN NORTH DEVON

Dennis Needham

Devon is a tourist paradise, but it's so easy to escape from the crowds – get off the beaten track to explore the delights of country walking and tiny Devonshire pubs in the company of a local expert!

£6.95

TEA SHOP WALKS IN SOUTH DEVON

Norman & June Buckley

This recent addition to our "Tea Shop Walks" series is a celebration of Devonshire afternoon teas, combined with thirty circular walks. Sections of the South West Coast Path are included, plus the lovely fringes of Dartmoor. Clear descriptions, accurate sketch maps and the authors' own stunning photographs make this an essential purchase for all those who love the easy life!

£6.95

All of our books are available from your local bookshop. In case of difficulty, or to obtain our complete catalogue, please contact:

**Sigma Leisure, 1 South Oak Lane, Wilmslow, Cheshire SK9 6AR
Phone: 01625 – 531035   Fax: 01625 – 536800
E-mail: sigma.press@zetnet.co.uk**

ACCESS and VISA orders welcome. Please add £2 p&p to all orders.

http://www.sigmapress.co.uk